Bamboo Son

Bamboo Son

A Hmong Refugee's Search for Identity and the American Dream

Pao Lor

WISCONSIN HISTORICAL SOCIETY PRESS

Published by the Wisconsin Historical Society Press
Publishers since 1855

The Wisconsin Historical Society helps people connect to the past by collecting, preserving, and sharing stories. Founded in 1846, the Society is one of the nation's finest historical institutions.
Join the Wisconsin Historical Society: wisconsinhistory.org/membership

Printed in the United States of America
Cover designed by Mayfly book design
Typesetting by John Ferguson

30 29 28 27 26   1 2 3 4 5

Library of Congress Cataloging-in-Publication Data
Names: Lor, Pao, 1972– author
Title: Bamboo son : a Hmong refugee's search for identity and the American dream / Pao Lor.
Other titles: Hmong refugee's search for identity and the American dream
Description: [Madison, Wisconsin] : Wisconsin Historical Society Press, [2026]
Identifiers: LCCN 2025040251 (print) | LCCN 2025040252 (e-book) | ISBN 9781976600654 paperback | ISBN 9781976600661 e-book
Subjects: LCSH: Lor, Pao, 1972– | Hmong Americans—Wisconsin—Biography | Immigrants—Wisconsin—Biography | Teachers—Wisconsin—Biography | Refugees—Laos—Biography | Refugees—Thailand—Biography | Wisconsin—Biography | LCGFT: Autobiographies
Classification: LCC F590.H55 L66 2026 (print) | LCC F590.H55 (e-book)
LC record available at https://lccn.loc.gov/2025040251
LC ebook record available at https://lccn.loc.gov/2025040252

♾ The paper used in this publication meets the minimum requirements of the American National Standard for Information Sciences—Permanence of Paper for Printed Library Materials, ANSI Z39.48-1992.

Contents

Introduction

On a July evening in 2023, I realized I was living alone for the first time in my life. I was fifty-one years old, and it was my first night in a small studio apartment in La Crosse. I looked through my east-facing window, but I couldn't quite make out Grandad Bluff through the dim light. Beyond that, about 175 miles away, my wife, Maya, and our four kids were in our house on the shore of the Fox River in Kimberly, Wisconsin. But I was here, alone, on the fourth floor of a brick apartment building, for the foreseeable future. I had never lived in a place of my own—not to mention a place far from friends, family, and the community that had become so familiar to me since moving to Wisconsin forty-four years earlier. To make it through each day and week, I knew I would need every ounce of my resilience and determination.

Several months earlier, I was offered the opportunity of a lifetime: a position as the associate dean of the School of Education at the University of Wisconsin–La Crosse. It was the culmination of decades of work as a teacher, professor, and administrator in Wisconsin schools and universities. I hated the idea of living away from my wife and children, but I felt that this was part of my destiny, or as we Hmong call it, kuv txoj hmoos. Ultimately, what made me decide to take on this new and lonely endeavor was Maya. She said to me, with a good dose of humor and realism:

> Treat it like when we were dating. You work throughout the week and then come to visit me during the weekend. Every

weekend is a getaway. Plus, just like when we were dating, it's only temporary. And look at what that sacrifice got you? Me. And look at where that sacrifice got us? The life that we have now. So, go on and do what you must do—like you always have. I'll be right here waiting. I'm not going anywhere, Pao. Just like then. We'll all be in a better place in a few years from now.

Even with Maya's support, I needed to add some inspirational ambience to my studio. That fall, I decorated the walls with family photos, artwork, inspirational quotes, calming beach scenes, and a battery-operated wooden clock. I oriented my desk to face the east, knowing that I would be facing both of my homes: Kimberly and Laos. In my small dining area, I arranged two chairs around my circular table, one for me and one for Maya when she visited. On a nearby end table, I placed my electric rice cooker and air fryer. In just four small living areas, I had everything I would need to work, eat, sleep, and stay driven toward my greater purpose.

As the weeks passed, I began to adjust to my new responsibilities and routines. I cooked at least three dinners per week, and I saved the leftovers for lunch. I tried to diversify my dinners, sometimes stir-frying salmon with vegetables, sometimes making soup with shrimp, sometimes air-frying chicken with asparagus and onions. Even after forty-four years in the United States, I hadn't yet adjusted to eating most meals without rice. I ate out about once a week, mostly at Hmong's Golden Egg Rolls on State Street. I usually ordered pho, fried Hmong sausage, Thai-style papaya salad, fried chicken thighs, sticky rice, pork egg rolls, or occasionally the fried tilapia. Of the many restaurants in the greater La Crosse area, Hmong's Golden Egg Rolls was most compatible with my aging palate. With my busy schedule, I greatly appreciated the proximity of the restaurant and the efficiency of my electric cooking appliances.

When I accepted the position of associate dean of the School of Education at the University of Wisconsin–La Crosse in 2023, I moved into this office. It amazes me to think of how much my life has changed since I was a child in the remote jungles of central Laos.

Given my appreciation for all these conveniences, I can only imagine how challenging life must have been for my parents as they were raising my siblings and me in isolated tribal villages in the jungles of central Laos. Even something as simple as starting a fire to prepare a meal must have been exhausting. Not only did they have to start each fire from scratch, but they also had to monitor it closely to prevent it from getting out of control and burning down our rice-thatched hut or, worse yet, the entire village. It would have been impossible for my parents to imagine me living the life I live now.

For the first several years of my childhood, I lived in a series of small villages in Laos with my parents and siblings. In 1977, when I was about five years old, we fled our home, fearing for our lives, and embarked on a dangerous journey to Thailand. Between about 1960 and 1975, many Hmong people—who also refer to themselves as Hmoob or HMoob—under the leadership of General Vang Pao and supported by the US Central Intelligence Agency, had been fighting communist Laotian and Vietnamese forces along the border of Laos and Vietnam. This covert military operation is now known as the Secret War. Following the United States' withdrawal from Vietnam in 1975, the Hmong were left to fend for themselves against the Pathet Lao and the Vietnamese. Thousands of Hmong fled their homes in Laos, journeying through jungles and mountains, hoping to reach Thailand and find refuge from the fighting.

For the Hmong who first fled Laos and made it to Thailand, many got a glimpse of their uncertain future in 1975 when the United States and other countries granted them relocation as refugees. That year, approximately 3,500 Hmong relocated to the United States. The delegate from the US State Department at the time may have wondered, "With all due respect to what the Hmong did to support the US in Laos over the last fifteen years, how can the Hmong—a semi-nomadic, shamanistic, agricultural, and mostly illiterate people—make it in the US, one of the most developed, modernized human civilizations?" I like to imagine a Hmong representative responding:

> I am Hmong. I am fluent in French, English, Lao, Vietnamese, and Thai. I have no doubt the Hmong will make it in the United States. Look at their commitment to succeed in life. They have farmed. They have supported and guided their families, villages, and communities for centuries. More important, they've fought and even died on behalf of the United States. They've persevered in the face of enemies, minefields, starvation, and many other tragedies. Is life in the United States any harder than what they have already

experienced, endured, and survived? This is the Hmong I know. I know the Hmong will succeed.

At first, my family stayed in Laos, assuming we were safe because my father had not fought alongside the Americans. However, after my father was assassinated in 1977, my mother, siblings, and I, along with two uncles and their families, left for Thailand. After weeks spent narrowly escaping starvation, disease, landmines, and other horrors along our trek, my mother and sister Shoua drowned while crossing the Mekong River—the final leg of the journey. At age six, I became an orphan.

My five surviving siblings and I endured two years of refugee life in two separate camps in Thailand: Ban Nong Khai and Ban Vinai. Though our time in the refugee camps was miserable, we never gave up hope that a better life was just around the corner. Ultimately, the mother-in-law of my eldest brother sponsored us, and we relocated to Long Beach, California, in 1980. Later that year, at age eight, I stumbled into an unexpected life in Green Bay, Wisconsin. The distance between my humble beginnings and where I am today has been littered with challenges as well as possibilities.

Bamboo Son is a follow-up to my first memoir, *Modern Jungles: A Hmong Refugee's Childhood Story of Survival.* When I wrote *Modern Jungles,* I shared a child's perspective of the Hmong American experience, from leaving my home in the jungles of central Laos in the 1970s to establishing a new home in Green Bay in the 1980s. As such, many memories shared in *Modern Jungles* are fragmented and simplistic, reflecting my psychological landscape as a young person—one shared by many Hmong Americans of my generation. We were both confused and curious, hopeful and uncertain.

At a young age, we witnessed and survived terrible atrocities. We also were exposed to diverse cultures, languages, and

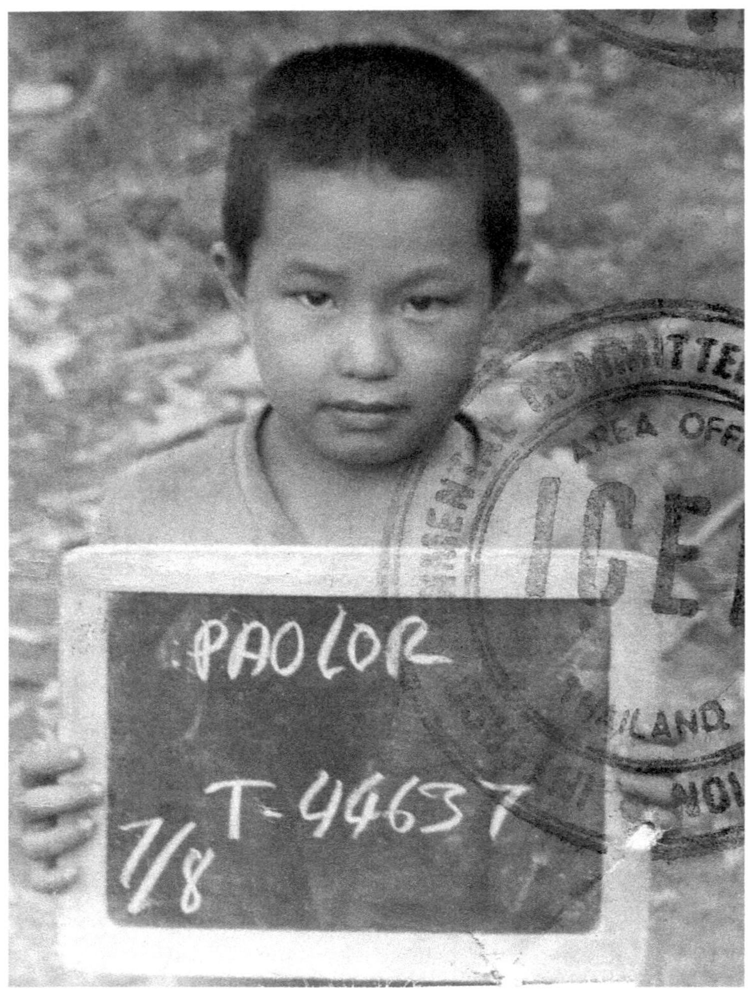

When I was about seven years old, I had my photo taken as part of the relocation process at Thailand's Ban Vinai refugee camp in 1979.

peoples. Consequently, we wanted to squeeze everything we could out of our new opportunity in the United States. Today, as a result of our ambition and resiliency, Hmong Americans have established communities in the US that demonstrate self-healing and nurturing, improving socioeconomic status and educational attainment, pride in our contributions to US culture and society, and appreciation of our history.

In *Bamboo Son,* I share my story from age fourteen to fifty-two—the journey of one man searching for his true identity and the American dream. In Hmong, the word *bamboo* or *ntsuag* has two meanings. It refers to the bamboo plant, which has many significant cultural and practical uses in Hmong life. The word also means orphan. Therefore, *bamboo son,* in Hmong, means *tub ntsuag* or *orphan son.* To survive and succeed as a Hmong orphan, like bamboo, one must be resilient and adaptable, bend without breaking, and stand tall against enormous odds.

It is my hope that this book invites readers to discover, appreciate, and embrace the diverse lived experiences of refugees, displaced peoples, and underprivileged groups. It is also my hope that *Bamboo Son* is a testament to the fierce kindness and unwavering generosity of people everywhere. Lastly, it is my hope that readers of this book will unearth some of the secret ingredients to living a fulfilling, transformative, and enriching life.

PART I

The Kickoff

Every human being is intended to have a character of his own; to be what no others are, and to do what no other can do.

—William Ellery Channing

1

Ntev, ntev, los lawm—a long, long time ago—I woke up, and it was still dark. My anxiety immediately took over. It was my first day of high school in September 1986, and I hadn't slept well. In fact, I hadn't been sleeping well for the past several weeks. With each passing day that brought me closer to the start of school, I became more and more unsettled.

This was primarily due to the nightmares. I'd started having them near the end of the last school year, and they'd only worsened over the summer. In one, bullies duct-taped me to one of the huge trees in front of Green Bay East High School. In another, they gave me wedgies while I walked down a hallway in between classes. In a third, a bunch of bearded seniors grabbed me and threw me headfirst into a giant plastic garbage bin. In yet another, I was an intimidated boy among fully developed young women who had sexual interests in freshmen like me.

Physically, I was vulnerable. I was newly aware that being five feet tall and weighing 110 pounds could impact my well-being. And unlike some of my stronger and bigger Hmong friends who could defend themselves, I cringed at the very idea of violence—both violence against me and, if necessary, me using violence against others.

Over the summer, to mentally prepare myself for the harassment I expected to encounter at school, I taught myself a few kung fu moves that I picked up from movies. But even with that preparation, I knew that I would likely choose flight over fight in any physically threatening situation. I could run fast—very fast. More importantly, I knew I could quickly achieve high speeds from a stationary position. It was sad that I had to rely on this ability for my own safety, but I knew some of my Hmong friends and classmates had even lower chances of escaping bullies than I did.

Worse yet, I was also psychologically vulnerable. I believed I was inferior to my peers who had parents, whose lives seemed much better than mine. I thought I was destined to fail and they were destined to achieve. I also believed my peers had unlimited support and that I had none. Up to this point in my life, I'd had to work hard to earn almost everything I had, and I didn't know how much more of that I could endure.

My life experiences had taught me that being a Hmong orphan was taboo. I had never met a successful person who had been an orphan. I did have a bit of hope, which came from a fairytale I'd heard many times in the Thai refugee camps of my childhood. In that story, an orphan boy is mistreated by his aunt, uncle, and fellow villagers, but he eventually ends up with a beautiful home and a generous wife and lives happily ever after. Even in that story, though, it took a magical princess from a magical kingdom to save the poor orphan boy. I figured that was unlikely to happen to me here, in modernized America.

Also, my English wasn't very good, and I literally took that to mean kuv yog ib tus neeg ruam, or that I was an unintelligent person. In junior high, if I could understand 60 percent of my teachers' instructions, I was happy, especially in my science, social studies, and English classes. I had fewer issues with art, gym, math, and other electives where I could rely on my visual, spatial, and physical abilities.

I didn't realize it at the time, but I did have a few attributes that would help me in this new environment: my work ethic, my ambition, my intuition, and, of course, my luck.

Over the summer, I had moved with my family from one Green Bay neighborhood to another—my seventh move in the six years

I'd been living in Green Bay since 1980. The process of acclimating to a new place now felt like an old habit. I lived with my youngest brother, Kong, who was twelve, as well as my older brother Vue, who was twenty-four; Vue's wife; and their two young children. My eldest brother, Vang, who was twenty-nine, and his family lived about a mile away, and my brother Pheng, who was nineteen, lived with them. My sister, Yanghoua, who was twenty-two, and her family were in California.

Our new place was one of four units at 416 South Webster Avenue, one of the busiest north–south streets on Green Bay's east side, running from the University of Wisconsin–Green Bay to Chicago Street in De Pere. Our unit was on the second floor and had three bedrooms. Vue's in-laws lived in the other upper unit. I had no idea who lived in the lower units. The building had originally been a single-family home, and I often thought about how the people who first lived there must have been very wealthy.

My room faced Webster Avenue, and it took about a month for me to become numb to the noise of the traffic. I rarely came across Vue or his family, and crossing paths with Kong was also a rarity. My room and Kong's room were in opposite corners of the unit, and though there was just a wall between us, I had to walk through the living room and kitchen to reach the door to his room. Even though we were at different stages of life, my siblings and I were all quite independent. We implicitly understood that because we were poor, we each needed to do whatever we could to take care of ourselves. I was so consumed with meeting my own basic needs that I honestly didn't think much about how my siblings or their families were doing.

Vue worked as a bilingual paraprofessional with the Green Bay Area Public School District, and I knew our rent, utilities, and groceries were paid for by his income, as well as the monthly welfare checks Kong and I received as court-recognized orphans. I didn't know all the details, but I understood enough. And I had a general sense of Vue's expectations for me: to do well in school, stay out of trouble, and be a good person. As long as he wasn't on my case, I figured I was meeting both his spoken and unspoken standards.

My summer routine was fairly simple: wake up, take a shower, leave the house to hang out with friends or cousins, come back home, cook dinner for myself, fall asleep, and repeat the process the next day. This routine was occasionally interrupted by things like laundry, grocery shopping, and shooting robins from my window with an air gun. I was a pretty good shooter, but it was all at very close range. If I hit a bird, I would run down to grab it from our driveway or yard, then I would prepare it, boil it, and eat it. This was all before I knew the robin was Wisconsin's state bird.

Every now and then, I'd join some family members for a memorable night watching wrestling at the Brown County Veterans Memorial Arena. I looked forward to the energy, the drama, and the larger-than-life characters—it was pure entertainment. I loved watching legends like Jimmy "Superfly" Snuka, "Rowdy" Roddy Piper, "Macho Man" Randy Savage, Ric Flair, and of course, Hulk Hogan. Seeing my uncle Bliapao and other Hmong elders connect with something so deeply rooted in mainstream American culture gave me a sense that a bridge between our two worlds could exist.

I also spent some of my days practicing with my band. For over a year, I had been the drummer for the best band in Green Bay and the surrounding area—or at least, that's what I believed. We were called Nrhiav Hlub, or Seeking Love. My cousins and their friends had started the band a few years earlier, and I had joined as a drummer the previous summer. We played a variety of popular Hmong songs, ranging from classic rock to New Wave, as well as a few contemporary American songs like "White Wedding" by Billy Idol and "Cheri Cheri Lady" by Modern Talking. We mainly played at events in Appleton and Green Bay and a few times in

In the mid-1980s, I played drums in a band, but privately I found joy in playing the guitar.

Wausau and Milwaukee. Most times, we were a guest band, but a few times we were the featured band, which was exhausting. On those occasions, we had to bring our equipment and were always the last to leave. My favorite things about being a drummer were setting the rhythm and playing at the back of the stage.

Being in a band provided me with an escape from summer boredom and a hectic academic schedule. It also gave me a valid reason to avoid attending shamanistic ceremonies, soul-calling rituals, weddings, and funerals. At these events, I was asked to assist clan members by cleaning, cooking, and sometimes holding chickens and pigs for sacrifice, and I often received tedious lectures about life's vices from elders. After participating in these events for several years, I was starting to find them increasingly incongruous with my identity. By being in a band, however, I could contribute to the Hmong community in a way that was more aligned with my values.

Soccer was another one of my summer pastimes. I was a member of the Green Bay Rowdies, a U-14 competitive team (for players fourteen and under) that played league games and tournaments in northeast Wisconsin. The previous summer, I'd played for the Green Bay Warriors, another U-14 team. It was my first experience playing organized soccer, and I quickly came to love the sport. A couple weeks before the start of high school, I tried out for the high school soccer team, the Green Bay East Red Devils. I had no idea what "trying out" for soccer meant, since I'd been invited to play for the Warriors and the Rowdies, but a few of my teammates had somehow convinced me to give it a shot. Ironically, none of them decided to try out. In fact, one of them had chosen to play hockey instead.

When I arrived at tryouts, I realized I knew no one there. Also, I was shocked by the size of the high school players. They were much bigger than most of my former teammates and rivals—also stronger, faster, and more skilled. When it came time to scrimmage, I couldn't keep up with anyone. I felt lost and dazed, like everything around me was a spinning blur. I was moving, but I was as useless as a cone. My speed and good instincts no longer camouflaged my weaknesses and inexperience. And my small stature didn't help.

Somehow, I endured tryouts day after day. But on each lonely bike ride home, I fixated on how poorly I was doing. I was especially confused hearing other players talk about making the "JV" or "varsity" teams. *What in the world are they talking about?* I wondered. *Why does making the JV or varsity team seem so important to them?* But I didn't dare ask anyone to explain it to me. Asking them would only empower my inner demons, who continued to convince me that I was intellectually, culturally, and physically inferior.

Nonetheless, quitting never crossed my mind. Somehow, something deep inside of me wanted to find out how it would end. After two weeks of tryouts, I learned I'd made the junior varsity team. Even though I had no idea what I had gotten myself into, I was extremely happy.

I was relieved to be a member of the JV team, but this did little to quell my nerves on the first day of school. My alarm went off at six o'clock. It felt way too early. But I needed to make it to my first class, which started at seven. When I'd picked my class schedule, I hadn't realized that probably 99 percent of my fellow classmates had chosen a first class that started at 7:45 a.m. Already needing more sleep, I wondered whether I could endure this new routine. I pictured my still-sleeping classmates. *Why am doing this to myself?* I asked. But I didn't have any answers.

Once I'd showered and dressed, I walked the five or so blocks from my house to East High School. The first leg was to the corner of Crooks Street and Webster Avenue and through the intersection heading east on Crooks. Then I turned left onto hilly South Clay Street and right onto Stuart Street before taking a left onto South Baird Street. From there, I could see East High. I felt a sense of comfort passing Washington Junior High School on the way. I'd gained a lot of confidence in academics and sports at that school last year. But of course, not everything there had been pleasant, especially the fight I'd gotten into with a bully in my gym class and the way he and his friends had harassed me and other Hmong students for the rest of the school year. I worried that the bully would end up in one or more of my high school classes.

When I stepped through the main entrance of East High School, it was the first time I'd set foot in the building. I'd had no tour or orientation, so I had no clue where I was going. With its empty halls, the place seemed almost haunted. *Where is everyone?* I thought. I would soon learn that I had arrived much earlier than most other students. I quickly figured out the room number sequence and climbed up a flight of stairs toward my first class, social studies. I knew the location and combination of my assigned locker, since I had received that information in the mail. But with the creepy vibe in the halls, I wasn't about to go there now.

When I entered the room of my first class, I was impressed to see that a few students had arrived even earlier than me. But I was also a bit disappointed. Apparently, their motivation to learn exceeded my own. I knew a few of them from the junior high track team. Our teacher, Mr. Boyle, looked old and wise. Just as the clock struck seven, he welcomed us and began sharing course information and expectations. By this point, I had become quite accustomed to the vast difference between how Americans and Hmong people view time. Many Hmong are very relaxed when it comes to being on time for events, while many Americans are quite rigid. At the end of class, we had a few minutes to chat with our fellow classmates, but I didn't participate. It was simply not my nature. Instead, I sat quietly, wondering, *Are my classmates smarter than me? What if I don't do well?* Finally, the bell rang, bringing me some much-needed relief.

Stepping out into the hallway, I now saw students everywhere, congregating, talking, opening and closing lockers, getting books and pencils, and heading in all directions. Many chatted in groups of two or more, although a few individuals stood by their lockers looking lonely. I remembered how lost and confused I felt on my first day at Washington Junior High last year. Thankfully, I now felt much more comfortable navigating the synchronized chaos of school.

The class routine for the rest of my day was the same, except for lunch. In the cafeteria, I finally met up with a few friends from last year. Most of them were outcasts like me. We really enjoyed each other's company. After comparing our schedules, I was dismayed to learn that, unlike last year, I wouldn't have any classes with them.

I continued through the rest of the day, wondering when my cultural and intellectual inferiority would be discovered. I experienced intense moments of anxiety when thoughts of my nightmares suddenly crossed my mind. I also worried about potential retaliation from last year's gym class bully and his friends. It wasn't until my last class when my fears finally subsided. Thankfully, the bully wasn't in any of my classes and neither were his friends. Also, my nightmares no longer seemed realistic. There had been no duct tape incidents, no wedgies, no garbage bin attacks, and no unwanted sexual advances. For the most part, everyone seemed to be minding their own business, and I didn't think that was going to change overnight.

As I walked home and then biked to soccer practice, I thought about how my classmates and I probably had similar hopes and fears about the year ahead. How each of us would manage them would depend on the life skills, knowledge, and dispositions we had acquired from our families, communities, and personal journeys thus far. In my case, surviving my journey from Laos to Thailand to the United States had hardened me in many ways. Though I was very independent, I knew the Hmong community provided me with a sense of safety, belonging, and purpose. At the same time, I was on a quest to discover myself and my place in the world. And as an orphan, I was, in many ways, a blank canvas.

Despite the hardships of my early years, I felt fortunate to be in the United States, a place where—with the synchronization of courage, motivation, natural abilities, and a bit of luck—I believed I could live a soul-enriching life. I knew I would have been deprived of this opportunity if my family had remained in Thailand and Laos. At age fourteen, I had already lived through many of the extremes the world had to offer. Yet I was unaware that my life had only just begun.

2

To my surprise, the first several weeks of high school passed rather quickly. Everything was novel and exciting, and I was relieved to find the experience much less terrifying than I had anticipated. I did share the halls with bearded seniors and fully developed young women, but for the most part, everyone was civil and pleasant. I minded my own business, and they minded theirs. As months went by, I became less anxious about being harassed, and my sense of belonging slowly began to solidify. When I received my progress report midway through the first quarter, I was ecstatic to have earned almost all As. However, I didn't share my grades with anyone. I wanted to do my best without seeking recognition or accolades.

Soccer, too, brought me much joy. I couldn't believe I almost hadn't tried out. Despite the uncertainty I felt during tryouts, my confidence increased once the season started. On the soccer field, I did things instinctively and experienced a kind of happiness that I hadn't found anywhere else. My coach showed his confidence in me by putting me in the central midfielder position, and I felt that my teammates respected me. Every day, I couldn't wait to step on the field to practice or play games, my escape from life's monotony at school and in the community.

Unfortunately, some of my Hmong friends and classmates found high school much more challenging. At social and cultural gatherings on the weekends, they told me stories of their fights and negative interactions with white bullies during school in the library and the hallways, and after school at Johannes Park across the street from East High. I came to realize that my rigid daily routine of school followed by soccer was shielding me from these darker experiences.

To end the season in late October, my team participated in a junior varsity tournament at the Broadview soccer fields in Allouez, a suburb of Green Bay. During one of the games, as I continued to steal the ball from my opponents and set up my teammates to score, I suddenly had a new awareness of my talent and abilities. I felt as if I could do whatever I wanted on the field and no opposing players could stop me. I'd never experienced such a rush of confidence before. In the end, our team easily won the tournament.

After the championship game, the varsity coach approached me and asked if I would join his team for their championship game, which was happening right after ours. I had only seen this coach at practice a few times before. I was surprised, elated, and afraid all at once. I had no idea what it meant to play on the varsity team, but still I replied, "Sure."

As I prepared for my fifth game of the day, I was full of adrenaline. My one goal during warm-ups was simply not to look stupid. When the game started, I was very relieved to find myself on the bench. At halftime, our team was leading one-zero. About ten minutes into the second half, we scored again. Two-zero. The coach then called my name and substituted me in. Even in my familiar central midfielder position, I was beyond nervous. When the opponent kicked off and play resumed, my nervousness was replaced with a feeling of bewilderment. The players moved at an incredibly fast pace. I received a pass, and then, as I controlled the ball and turned to face the defenders, an opponent steamrolled me into the cold, slushy grass. Where had he come from? I'd never been pummeled so thoroughly and painfully.

A foul was called. And as soon as play resumed, all was forgotten. But I still felt lost. The pummeling hadn't knocked any sense into me. I spent the rest of my time on the field determined not let the opponent score. When we won two-zero, I mostly felt relieved.

When winter arrived—abruptly, as it often did in Green Bay—I realized I still hadn't gotten used to it, and I didn't think I ever would. The extreme weather and changing seasons were nothing like the climate where I'd grown up in Laos and Thailand. Though the long months of cold temperatures were similar in some ways to the rainy seasons of Southeast Asia, I found it much more challenging to cope with the snow and extended darkness.

Still, even in the cold weather, I had come to value my dark morning walks to school. During that time, I could be at peace with myself and with the world. Occasionally, when the temperature dropped below zero, I had to ask Vue for a ride to school. I hated to inconvenience him, but walking would have been a death wish. Though Vue still had to go to work after dropping me off, he never complained.

In December, I snapped out of my early winter blues when my band members and I decided to go to St. Paul. We weren't going there to play but rather to attend the Noj Peb Caug, or Hmong New Year, gathering. We would check out the quality of the bands playing at the festivities—and check out the single young women as well. I looked forward to the trip, because I had never been to St. Paul and I heard that there were a lot of Hmong people there. But I was also a bit nervous. Members of the Hmong community said that diseases, particularly kas cees or STDs, were rampant in big cities like St. Paul and easily spread from one person to another. We were told not to sit on any public toilets or make physical contact with any strangers.

Our group consisted of me, my cousin Ger, my brother Pheng, and our friends Yia and Chao, who were half brothers. With Ger at the wheel, we drove seven hours on Highway 29 through Wausau, Chippewa Falls, and a few other towns and cities before we merged onto Highway 94. When we finally reached St. Paul, we drove through the downtown area before heading to our cousin's house. I had never seen so many Black people or been in such a congested space surrounded by so many tall buildings. Prior to this, I had interacted with just two Black people in my life: my classmates Roosevelt and Cornelius. Cornelius and I had met earlier in the school year, and we quickly became friends. He shared that he had moved from Detroit to Chicago to Green Bay. He never mentioned anything about his family and neither did I. One time, at lunch, however, he did share with me that he hated the sound of the bell that went off in between classes.

Curious, I asked him, "Why?"

"It's because I used to box," he replied. "And the sound makes me jump. It makes me think it's the next round." I appreciated him sharing something so personal. Though a part of me wanted to laugh, I could sense the seriousness of his admission and instinctively restrained myself. I had similar physical reactions to anything that sounded like gunfire or bombs due to my early experiences amid war in Laos. For that reason, the Fourth of July and I hadn't been the best of friends. But I didn't share this with anyone, not even Cornelius.

I was relieved when we finally headed to our cousin's place, which was a unit in the St. Paul public housing project called McDonough Homes. At the time, I thought it was McDonald Homes because nobody I knew could pronounce it correctly. I didn't know anything about the geography of St. Paul, but with no other houses or neighborhoods around, the development felt isolated from the rest of the city. With some daylight left, our cousin showed us around. Since arriving in the United States, I had never been around so many Hmong people. They were everywhere, entering and leaving various units and walking in all directions. We visited a few of our cousin's friends and neighbors. Being around so many Hmong people, and especially seeing their altars and other cultural items, brought back my memories of living in Ban Vinai and Ban Nong Khai.

The next day, we woke early and went to the St. Paul Civic Center for the Hmong New Year festivities. The indoor arena was huge and absolutely full of Hmong people. Many wore traditional Hmong clothes, like embroidered shirts, red sashes, and black aprons, while most of the younger generation wore the latest fashions, such as high-waisted jeans and shirts with shoulder pads. We avoided the crowd and sat at the very top of the arena. While some band members roamed around, I stayed put. I really enjoyed being alone, watching the competitions in dancing, singing, and traditional music happening on the giant stage below. Even when I had no idea what was going on, I was mesmerized by the sights, sounds, activities, and aura.

Later that afternoon, we returned to our cousin's place to change clothes, then drove back to the Civic Center for the evening's party. This time, we sat closer to the stage and dance floor. As with other parties I had attended, most of the single young women sat in chairs near the dance floor, waiting for guys to ask them to dance. From a distance, I thought they all looked very pretty in their colorful party dresses. But with so many layers of make-up on their faces, I couldn't tell who was authentically attractive.

I had never been fond of this type of courtship ritual, and this evening was no different. I wasn't good at making small talk or dancing. I had only danced a few times, and all had been slow dances. At our band's debut in Oshkosh a year earlier, I'd shared a slow dance with a girl in a red dress named Maya. Maya and I hadn't had the chance to meet up again, but that first encounter had been so meaningful that I found myself measuring my interactions with other girls against it. I'd had a few other enjoyable moments with girls at local parties in Green Bay. So when a slow song started, despite my anxiety, I figured, *Why not? Let's give it a try here in St. Paul. I might never make it up here again.*

The rows of young women weren't that far away, but the walk there seemed to take forever. By the time I got close, most had already been escorted to the dance floor by other young men. I gathered my courage and asked a girl who was still waiting. The slow dance turned out to be almost intolerably long. She had cold hands, and even a cold waist, and I felt completely disconnected from her as we moved to the music. My experiences dancing with Maya and the other girls had been completely different. The awkwardness of our interaction, and my disappointment, deterred me from any more dancing that night. But the evening went by very quickly. I particularly enjoyed watching the bands perform. I focused on the drummers and their impressive skill in maintaining the rhythm.

On our drive back to Green Bay, I reflected on the gathering. Despite being surrounded by so many Hmong people, I still felt disconnected from my Hmong identity. I'd spent the first eight years of my life surrounded by Hmong people in Laos and Thailand, but I was coming of age in a predominantly white American community. I didn't know exactly where I belonged.

One-three-one zone. Two-three zone. Man to man. Collapse the zone. Help out. Switch. Close in. I had no idea what these terms meant. All I knew about basketball, and all that mattered to me about basketball, was dribbling, shooting, guarding, and running like hell.

But after my positive high school soccer experience, and now knowing what "trying out" meant, I figured I would try out for the freshman basketball team. I'd played basketball for the last two school years. Also, Mr. Larson, the coach, had been my science teacher at Washington Junior High. To my surprise, I made the team. However, all of my teammates had gotten a lot bigger, faster, and better since eighth grade. At the time, I had no idea how that had happened. Later, I discovered that while I had been busy playing soccer, working, and attending Hmong cultural events, they had been going to summer basketball camps and open-play sessions at school.

By late January, about halfway through the season, I still hadn't set foot on the court during a game, even though I'd attended every practice. This was a new experience for me. After warm-ups, I sat at the end of the bench, almost as if I didn't exist, until it was time to shake hands with the opponents at the end of the game. Though I had been elated to be on the bench at the start of the varsity soccer championship game, this experience of never moving from the bench was starting to wear on me.

One day, Coach Larson asked me to keep stats. Shocked, I thought, *What? I don't even know the game. How can I keep statistics?* But I said yes. As I tried to record everything, I realized I had no idea whether a missed shot was a turnover or not. At the end of the game, Coach Larson looked over my stats and lectured the team for having more turnovers than usual. Only I knew that the stats were likely incorrect. When I got home that evening, I made my decision. The next day, after school, I went to Coach Larson's office and turned in my uniforms. I didn't say a word, and neither did he. I took that to mean we were both glad I was gone.

Luckily, I still had soccer—even in the winter. Shortly after the high school soccer season ended, I'd been invited to join a U-16 travel team made up of players from different high schools. I'd moved up an age group, but most of my friends from the summer had stayed back on the U-14 team. I didn't know anyone, but I was still very excited. I loved our new uniforms and warmups, even though they didn't fit me well. The dark blue warmups brushed the ground unless I rolled them up at the waist, and the white shorts draped a bit beyond my knees.

Our coach, Fernando, seemed to understand my circumstances. I knew he had come from a different country, but I wasn't sure which one. My knowledge of the world was very limited. He walked and ran awkwardly because one of his legs was shorter than the other. I was curious to know what had happened to him, but out of respect, I never asked. Coach Fernando provided me with many resources so that I wouldn't stand out from my teammates. For instance, when we played in out-of-town tournaments, he discreetly gave me money so I could purchase food and drinks. I greatly appreciated his generosity.

In January, we started our season with an indoor series of games at the YMCA on Broadview Drive in Allouez. Once, we had a night game at eight o'clock, and I couldn't find a ride. Knowing that it would take me at least an hour to walk there, I left my house and started walking around six thirty. When I was about halfway there, it started snowing. I enjoyed the peaceful walk through various neighborhoods along the way, especially with the snow falling all around me.

After the game, I began walking home around nine o'clock. One of my teammate's parents had offered me a ride, but I told them I already had one. The reality was that I didn't want to trouble them, and I didn't want them to know where I lived. The snow had been accumulating for hours by that point. Again, I enjoyed walking through the neighborhoods, which were now covered in snow, and I almost wished the peaceful walk would never end. But I started to feel my toes in my black Mitre indoor soccer shoes become numb in the freezing cold, and I still had a quarter of the way left to go. That night, I learned that physical needs often supersede spiritual ones and that perfect moments are often brief.

3

In the summer of 1987, my soccer team played our first game at Memorial Park in Appleton. We wore our red and black jerseys with our white shorts. During the game, several opponents started making fun of my oversized shorts. I wanted to retaliate but managed to control my frustration. I didn't want to repeat what I'd done two years ago when I got a yellow card for taunting an opponent and kicking the ball at his face. I felt some satisfaction at the end of the game when I'd scored two goals, and they hadn't scored at all.

In mid-June, I left the team to attend a three-week precollege program at the University of Wisconsin–Oshkosh. Coach Fernando needed me, but he also knew how much education meant to me. My teammates' parents supported my decision as well and often gave me rides to games and tournaments. One time, an opponent grabbed the neck of my jersey and ripped a seam across the upper right shoulder. One of the parents sewed it together for me. I even got to ride in a Mercedes once, when my teammate Nathan's parents drove me home from a game. The smooth ride and the elegant white leather interior were like nothing I had ever experienced. Most members of the Hmong community purchased used Toyotas and American-made vehicles from the 1970s. While riding with Nathan and his parents, I wondered, *What do these people do for a living? What does a car like this cost? Is this kind of decadence only available to white people?*

In early July, the team headed to Indiana and Illinois for several tournaments, but I didn't travel with them. I simply didn't have the money. Plus, I had never done anything like that before.

Since I was home, which was relatively rare, some of my cousins invited me on a weekend trip to St. Paul to attend the largest Hmong festival in the country. I agreed, knowing I wouldn't need much money for the trip.

Sixteen of us left Green Bay around seven o'clock in the evening on Friday. We traveled in three vehicles: a conversion van and two Toyota Celicas. I ended up in the back row of the conversion van with my cousin Yang at the wheel. On Highway 29 around ten o'clock, Yang suddenly braked and exited. The driver behind him did the same, but the last driver rear-ended him. The damage was minimal, but because of the accident, we didn't arrive at my relative's house in St. Paul until around two in the morning.

We got up around seven to head to the festival, which was being held on the grounds of a school. I was shocked to see so many Hmong people and vendors. I noticed people playing soccer, volleyball, and sepak takraw, a sport similar to volleyball that is popular in Southeast Asia. Yang told us to meet back at the entrance around five o'clock.

I wanted to check out the vendors, but something Yang had told me on the drive to St. Paul was echoing in my head—one of the vendors might be the man who had ordered an assassin to kill my father in Laos. The man was one of the Chaofa leaders. Since moving to the United States, my family and I hadn't felt threatened or fearful of retaliation from the Chaofa. If we had remained in Laos, our feelings and actions might have been different. When Yang had shared this, I asked him, "Are the Chaofa still fighting in Laos?"

"Yes," Yang told me. "They continue to fight because they are hoping that one day the mighty Americans will come back to finish off the communists."

"Really? And do they really believe that?" I asked.

"Yes, they really believe that. Some even believe they are

invincible because they called themselves Chaofa, which means *princes of the sky* in Laotian."

"Really?"

"Yes, really! Well, at least, until they have lost that invincibility."

"So, how do they know when they have lost that invincibility?"

"When they go to battle and get killed."

I thought about it. "That doesn't make any sense," I said.

"Well, maybe not to you," Yang said, "but it makes sense to them."

After that conversation, I felt unsettled as I ventured into the vendor area of the school grounds. People sold herbal medicines, T-shirts, silver bars and coins, cooking pots, knives, food, and many other items. Every time I passed a male vendor in his thirties or forties, I worried that he could be the person who had ordered my father's assassination. At the same time, I knew I wouldn't recognize the man even if he was there. *Let it go, Pao. Let it go,* I thought, trying to calm myself.

By noon, I was starving, so I bought a bowl of pho from a vendor. It was hearty and filling. As I roamed the sidelines of the soccer games, I ran into Yang and stayed with him to watch a few games. I had attended smaller Hmong soccer tournaments in Wisconsin before but none like this one, which included some of the best Hmong and non-Hmong Asian soccer players in the United States. I'd heard that some of the players had played either in the army or in college back in Laos. In the late afternoon, we heard Team Wisconsin would soon be playing a team from Wausau, so we immediately went to that field. Yang and I joined a group of spectators on the sideline near where the Wausau team was warming up. I realized I knew two of their players—one lived in Green Bay and the other had previously lived in Green Bay. In fact, I had played pickup games with them a few times at Fort Howard Park.

As the Wausau team warmed up, we overheard a few players

telling the coach that they weren't sure if they were going to be able to play due to injuries. Out of nowhere, Yang said, "He can play!" Of course, he was pointing at me. It was just like Yang to call me out. *Nah,* I thought. *I'm not interested. Not at all.* But to my surprise, the coach told me to dress up.

"What position do you play?" he asked.

"Central midfielder, but I don't have any cleats," I replied, trying to get out of the mess.

"What size do you wear?" he followed up.

"Seven or eight?"

He looked around and grabbed a pair of Puma King cleats. "Here. These should fit."

Okay, I thought. *That was a quick solution.* "I also need shin guards and socks." Maybe I could still get out of this. But no, sure enough, some shin guards and socks suddenly materialized. The cleats fit surprisingly well. I didn't ask for shorts because I loved what I had on, a pair of colorful board shorts.

When the game began, I was glad to be on the sideline. Never before had I played at a Hmong tournament or with adults at this competitive level. But just before the start of the second half, the coach told me to go in. One of their central midfielders couldn't continue. I felt like a nervous wreck but tried not to let it show. Once the game resumed, all my nervousness vanished. Now, all that mattered was trying my hardest to win.

To my surprise, I played for the entire second half, and the game was tied zero–zero at the end of regulation play. Then, we won the shootout to advance in the tournament. I felt amazing about our win and relieved that I hadn't been asked to take a penalty kick. Our next game was the following day, and I was told to arrive early.

When I met the other players on the field the next morning, I learned we would be playing a Laotian team, and I would be starting. This made me extremely nervous, but again, I tried to hide my feelings. As we took our positions, I sized up the Laotian players. *Whoa*, I thought. *These players are much bigger than the ones I played against yesterday*. They were muscular and intimidating. Fortunately, my speed and agility neutralized some of their advantages. Again, the game ended zero–zero, and we had another shootout. Again, we won. I was elated. I learned that one more win would bring us to the finals.

In the semifinal game, we played a team from Minnesota. The players were tall and from various ethnic groups. I found their black uniforms very intimidating, and when I was told some of the players were gangsters, I could feel my spine tingling. But once again, all my uncertainty and fear vanished at kickoff, as though I'd teleported to a different universe. I played extremely well. My speed, fluidity, and raw talent made my age and lack of experience irrelevant. I even scored one of our team's two goals on a rebound after the opponent's goalkeeper failed to secure our direct free kick from about thirty yards out. We were now moving on to the championship game.

Around seven that evening, the sky suddenly darkened, and it looked as though it could rain at any moment. Packed together like sardines, fans filled the two sidelines and backlines. The hillside was crowded, as well. Some of the sideline spectators stood inches from the field. As the dark gray clouds began drizzling, I smiled at the irony of our opponents being named the Minnesota Lightning. They had some of the best players from Minnesota, California, North Carolina, Rhode Island, and Wisconsin.

Unlike our prior games, there was a certain formality to the championship game. We lined up on our half of the sideline and walked to the corner of the sideline and centerfield line to meet up with the other team. Then, both teams walked side by side to the center of the field. Once at centerfield, we veered to our side, and they veered to theirs. The tournament director and his crew approached each team, thanked us for making the tournament a success and for our sportsmanship, wished us luck, and asked us to please return to support the tournament next year. We then bowed once to the fans in front of us and once to the fans behind us.

After we jogged back to our sideline, our team members gathered to go over positions and basic strategies. I jogged onto the field to take my central midfield position and waited for kickoff. Despite my nervousness, I tried to soak in the moment. The fans. The weather. My teammates. Our opponents. The officials. The anticipation. The anxiety. The unknown. It was a thrilling moment—one I would come to cherish in retrospect.

In a flash, kickoff teleported me into the organic flow of the game, and I did all that I could to prevent the opponent from scoring. No more spectators. No more weather. No more anxiety. I would have been oblivious to a fan calling my name or even spitting at me. The game ended one–one. We lost the shootout, but I knew I played well. No opponent got by me, and I assisted on our one exciting goal. I took a corner kick and sent the ball to the far post where one of our players volleyed it into the back of the net. We took second place and were awarded a trophy, along with seven hundred dollars. I had no idea how privileged I was to be playing in the finals of such a prestigious soccer tournament at age fifteen. I didn't know it then, but I wouldn't return to the finals again until 2022, when I played in the fifty-plus age bracket.

About a month after this memorable experience, the coach invited me and another player from Green Bay to celebrate our achievement in Wausau. It was a family picnic at a local park. The team had used some of the prize money to purchase a cow for the occasion. The food—which included steaks, rare meat salad, sticky rice, sirloin tips, and tendon soup mixed with bitter gall bladder juice—was delicious. As we left that day, the coach thanked us and gave us each twenty dollars. I was elated. For a fifteen-year-old like me, with no source of income, twenty dollars meant a lot.

4

"Why you late, man?" asked one of my friends. It was September 1987, the first day of my sophomore year of high school, and the first time I had ever been late to lunch. Little did I know that I'd be late to lunch for the entire first semester. As I sat down to eat my pizza in the last ten minutes of the period, I shared my schedule with my friend:

7–7:40 a.m.—Social Studies

7:45–8:45 a.m.—Math

8:50–9:50 a.m.—Biology

9:55–10:55 a.m.—French II

11 a.m.–12 p.m.—College Prep Language Arts

12:05–12:45 p.m.—Gym

12:45–1 p.m.—Lunch

1:05–2:05 p.m.—Civics

2:10–3:10 p.m.—Typing I

"What is this? This is your schedule!" he laughed. "You must be a fool, stupid, or smart, Pao."

Not too witty and not very fond of small talk, I smiled and left it at that. I had no grandiose plan with my schedule. I just wanted to be busy at school. After school, I'd go to soccer practice, go home, sleep, wake up, do my homework, and go to school again.

Just like the last school year. Having a busy routine made me feel like I was doing something meaningful with my life.

Even if my lunch period was short, I felt glad to have time with the friends I'd made last year. We even met at our old lunch table—our sacred space. Almost all of us were misfits and outcasts. Jonathan hung out with us because we didn't care about his facial abnormalities, which remained even after a few surgeries, and his awkward walking posture. Cheng had a dirty mind and always had something inappropriate to say, whether it was about the food on our plates or the cheerleaders at the next table. Tong was married with a child on the way. While this may have seemed unusual to our white peers, it wasn't atypical for the Hmong students like me, Tong, and Cheng. Tong's wife, who was also a student at East, sometimes joined us, but she was easily put off by our immature jokes and topics of conversation. Sam mostly kept quiet and smiled at Cheng's dirty jokes, though he would sometimes say something brilliant that would make us all laugh. And me? I didn't chime in very often, and I was so thankful that everyone accepted my introverted nature. I knew no other school cliques had anything on us, because our friendship was judgment-free. Without speaking it aloud, we knew we all had it tough in our different ways.

Something else was different about the start of this school year: I had a girlfriend. Duene and I met over the summer attending the precollege camp at UW–Oshkosh, and we hit it off right away. She had a Hmong father and a Laotian mother, and she lived in Berlin, a small town a little over an hour away from Green Bay. She was a year older than me, elegant, well-dressed, and slender. During those three weeks, Duene and I formed a strong bond. We ate together, walked to classes together, and spent our evenings with each other. Since then, I'd visited her a few times when my soccer games brought me near Berlin, but we mostly kept in touch by talking on the phone and writing letters.

~

Like the previous year, soccer kicked off a few weeks before school started. This year, I didn't bother trying out for the varsity team. I looked forward to playing for the junior varsity team. Also, I hadn't forgotten about being pummeled to the ground in the second half of the varsity championship game last season.

After a few weeks of practices and two junior varsity games, however, I realized playing soccer wasn't fun anymore. This had nothing to do with my teammates or coaches and more to do with my sense that I was no longer being challenged. I enjoyed setting up my teammates so that they could score but not much else. I especially wanted our only female player to score. She worked so hard, and because she played the same position as me, she didn't get many opportunities.

After one game in particular, I felt my unhappiness becoming depressive. I walked slowly to the parking area where I had chained my bike. I had tuned out everything around me—the varsity team practicing in the distance, my teammates heading home, and the cars entering and leaving the parking lot. I just wanted to get home.

All of a sudden, I heard someone yell, "Pao!"

I stopped unlocking my bike and looked up. It was the varsity head coach. I hadn't seen him since last fall when he'd invited me to play in the varsity championship game. He was breathless, having run all the way from where the varsity team was practicing. He got right to the point.

"I'd like you to play on the varsity team," he told me. "You would be an excellent addition. And we could really use you." I was speechless. "Look, Pao, let's put it this way," he continued. "The way you play, I guarantee you will be one of the best players in the conference. You will easily make the all-conference team."

I was still unresponsive. I had no idea what the all-conference team was, and I found it hard to believe that I could be one of the best players at the varsity level. But I understood from the tone of his voice that he needed me. "Yeah, sure," I replied.

"Okay, great," he said. "See you tomorrow. Come and practice with the team."

"Sounds good, Coach. Thanks. See you tomorrow," I responded. But as he walked away, all I could think was that I wasn't sure what I had just gotten myself into—again.

I biked home as usual. What had just happened didn't cross my mind the rest of the way home. I just wanted to enjoy the ride home, get some rest, wake up early to do my homework, and enjoy my morning walk to my seven o'clock class. Though I wasn't conscious of it then, my early experiences in Laos and Thailand had taught me to cope with my reality by focusing on the present and not dwelling on the past or the future.

After joining the varsity team as a central midfielder, I quickly adjusted to the faster pace. My play became more fluid and assertive as the season went on. Before long, I felt completely reinvested in soccer. When the season ended, our record was six wins, one loss, and one draw, but I was disappointed that we placed second in the final conference standings due to our one loss.

The team had an end-of-season banquet in November. I didn't ask any of my family members to attend. In fact, my family members hadn't attended any of my games, either. I was still learning to navigate American norms and customs—plus, my independence was an important part of my identity. Instead, I invited my friend Timothy to the banquet. During dinner, Coach told me that he had advocated for me to be the conference player of the year, but a player from one of the private schools had won the award. This seemed to confirm my assumption that rich, smart, and talented kids attended private schools, while poor, less intelligent, less talented kids like me attended public school.

One day, during my language arts class, I was called to the main office. Usually, this was not a good sign. Because the language arts class was a college preparatory course, I believed it was full of ambitious students who all had a bright future ahead of them. I hated the feeling of those students looking at me and wondering, *What did you do, Pao?* I hadn't been to the main office since eighth grade, when I fought the bully in gym class. That visit had been most unpleasant.

When I got there, a man I'd never met was waiting for me. "You're Pao?" he asked.

"Yeah," I replied, disinterestedly. I was so engrossed in my daily school activities that any disruption to my routine was a major annoyance.

"Well, congratulations," he said. I had no idea what he was congratulating me for, but I didn't ask and didn't show any emotion. "Do you mind if we go out to the hallway to take some photos?" he asked.

I shrugged, "Sure, why not."

After he took some pictures, I returned to the main office and then to class. About a week or so later, one of my teachers handed me a newspaper. I had never touched a newspaper before, but I realized it was the sports section. I looked at it, and there I was. My headshot was arranged alongside headshots of ten other students and a coach.

My first thought was, *What? That's what I look like?* I could barely recognize myself. My family hadn't taken any pictures for a while, and we didn't have any full-length mirrors in our house. I probably hadn't taken a good look at myself for a few years. I read the article. Apparently, I had made the all-conference soccer team as a midfielder. I remembered that the varsity coach had predicted this months ago. I still had no idea what it meant to make the all-conference team, but I knew it was an honor. After class, I put the newspaper in my locker and went on with my day. When I finally got home, I stashed the article in a shoebox where I kept other items that were valuable to me, like a small gold necklace Vue had gifted me and a sportsmanship plaque I had been awarded when I played for the Warriors. At the time, I couldn't grasp that my coach and teammates, not to mention many Hmong individuals who'd seen me on the cover of the sports section, likely felt pride in my accomplishment. What mattered to me wasn't the recognition but the sense of fulfillment.

Though I did well in soccer that fall, I was disappointed to discover I was no longer in a band. We hadn't been practicing as usual, and one day I asked one of the members why. He told me the older members had gotten into a dispute and disbanded. They had already divided up the equipment and money, which wasn't much.

"Why wasn't I told?" I asked.

"I don't know," he answered.

I had no stake in the money or equipment, but it would have been nice to be informed. On the positive side, I hadn't been involved in the dispute and was able to maintain good relationships with my former bandmates.

During that first semester, with school and soccer occupying much of my days, I usually didn't get home until eight or nine o'clock at night. By then, I was physically and mentally drained. For the first month or so, I tried to complete my homework before heading to bed, but that wasn't effective. To solve the problem, I returned to completing as much homework as possible at school—during lunch and other available minutes of free time—and then waking up early to complete the rest. That worked well, because each morning, I felt replenished and energized.

After the end of the first quarter, I earned high marks in all of my classes except biology. Most of the time, I had no idea what Mr. Adamson was talking about. The tests were long and multiple choice, and they were often written in academic language that was unfamiliar to me. Everyone in the class did horribly, except for two classmates I had known since eighth grade, David and John. David got a B and John got an A. I almost failed with a D+. Heading into the second quarter, I wasn't confident that my grade would improve. I heard that many parents had complained about the class, but nothing came out of it.

Because of the D+, I especially didn't want to share my quarter grades with Vue. But I hadn't been sharing my grades with him for several years now. I knew he had been burdened with caring for Kong and me for years, and I didn't want to add anything to the load he was already carrying. Vue had been about thirteen when our father was assassinated and fourteen when our mom drowned. He'd always been diminutive for his age, due to being malnourished. In contrast to Vue, Vang, my eldest brother, had often been out of the family picture. From an early age, he sought ways to distance himself from our parents and older siblings. As a teenager, he left our family to move with friends to Laos's capital city, Vientiane, and eventually Nongkhai, Thailand. He had always carved out his own path away from the family, but he never neglected his obligation to support us when we needed it. Though each of us was in a different phase of life and we mostly kept to ourselves, the six of us were always there for each other, without question.

After soccer ended, I had planned to take driver's education, but now with a D+ on my report card, I wasn't so sure if Vue would let me. Once I had my driver's license and a car, I would be able to do many things I couldn't currently do, including visit my girlfriend, Duene, in Berlin. For Christmas, she had given me a beautiful, colorful sweater, and I'd given her a necklace with a half of a broken heart pendant. I had the other half. I had been wearing the sweater at least once a week.

One evening, without telling Vue about the biology grade, I gathered up my courage and asked, "Do you mind if I take driver's education?"

"Yes, sure," Vue replied. "How much does it cost and where will you be taking it?" Back when I was in fifth grade, Vue had painfully knuckled my head, and I had never forgotten it. But since then, he had been very supportive of me and my pursuits, like soccer, the band, academics, and other sports. As an orphan, I knew I was fortunate to have an outstanding brother like Vue to care for me.

"Ninety-nine dollars," I told him, "and it's just down the block on Crooks Street. It's after school, so it wouldn't interfere with my classes. Plus, I don't have soccer anymore. And I can just walk there and walk back home."

He said, "I will have a check ready for you to take with you on your first day." I was happy with his response, especially because our family's finances were a mystery to me. I knew Vue worked as a paraprofessional for the Green Bay Area Public School District, but I wasn't aware of his earnings. I also knew Kong and I received a monthly allowance from Social Services as wards of the court, but I didn't know the exact amount. Past experiences—like the times he'd bought me soccer cleats and new clothes at the start of each school year—had taught me that if I needed money for something important, he would find a way to provide it.

Sure enough, Vue wrote a check for me to take on my first day. I was excited to learn, and knowing that Vue had sacrificed money for me to take the course only heightened my focus and effort. About eight of us were in the class. Our instructor was personable and made the hours, days, and weeks pass quickly. She explained rules and good driving habits in a way that resonated with us adolescents. Her teaching methods were so effective that we all passed our written test.

My first road lesson came in late February, and it was snowing. I met my driving instructor at our driveway, and I was glad to see that it was the same instructor from our classes. Since I was the first student to be picked up, she told me to get behind the wheel.

She instructed me to back out of my driveway into the rush-hour traffic on Webster Avenue. I was beyond nervous. Other than the few times I'd driven my cousin's car about ten yards in a cucumber field, this was the first time I had ever been behind the wheel of an automobile.

Very slowly, I backed out and got us on the road. We headed south toward De Pere then made some turns until we reached a quiet neighborhood. For the next twenty minutes or so, I drove around the quiet streets of beautiful neighborhoods where I knew only rich white Americans resided. Once, I didn't release the steering wheel as I turned, and I almost crashed the car into an embankment of snow. Luckily, I avoided a full-on crash. Soon, we picked up a few other students, and I was very relieved to let them drive.

After I'd completed the required hours of lessons, I immediately scheduled my road test for April 5, the earliest date I could take it. A few weeks before the test, Vue took me out for some driving practice in our 1985 Ford Escort. We started in the parking lots at Northeast Wisconsin Technical College and UW–Green Bay before I went on the road. I found learning to drive a manual quite challenging.

Several hours before my scheduled road test, Vue picked me up from school. He drove us to our cousin's house to borrow his automatic maroon Toyota Corolla; I did not want to drive a manual for the test. After two more hours of driving practice, I felt confident and prepared. And I was motivated to pass on my first attempt because if I didn't, I'd have to wait another several months to retake it.

After I checked in at the DMV, the examiner and I walked out to the car. We checked that the brake lights, headlights, and turn signals were all working properly before heading off. At the examiner's direction, I drove around the Lombardi and Oneida area, then got on the highway.

Once we returned to the DMV, the examiner went over my performance with me. My speed, turns, and highway driving were good. I had remembered to check my side and rearview mirrors, as well as my blind spots. I had obeyed the traffic lights and signs on our drive. The one thing I hadn't aced was parallel parking. But I had passed the test overall.

"Congratulations, son!" the examiner exclaimed. I was elated.

Once I had my license, Vue started letting me drive the Escort. I was glad I hadn't needed to beg him for it, because I had heard horror stories from some of my friends about how they got their cars. Some threatened their parents by saying they would get married, run away, or join a gang if they didn't get a car.

For the next few months, I struggled to master driving a manual. I had trouble getting out of first gear, stopping on hilly roads, and multitasking in various traffic situations. In fact, sometimes my driving was downright unsafe. To improve my skills, I often waited until eleven o'clock at night when there was no traffic, drove downtown where I could find one-way streets, and worked on my driving skills in a safe environment. Those were late nights, but I was determined to master the task, and eventually, I did.

5

"You could graduate next year if you want," Mr. Dernbach, my counselor, told me at our spring meeting after looking over my credits.

"Are you sure?" I asked.

"Yes," he confirmed. "By the end of this semester, you will have fourteen and a half credits, and you need twenty and a half credits to graduate. So, you just need six more. That shouldn't be too hard, since you took seven credits your freshman year and seven and a half your sophomore year."

"Okay," I responded, still trying to process the news. "What classes do I need to take to make that happen?"

Mr. Dernbach outlined the classes I needed, including chemistry, social studies, math, physical education, and two credits of language arts.

"Two credits in language arts. What should I take there?" I asked.

"You could do composition in the first semester and speech in the second semester," he suggested. "Writing and speaking in public aren't bad skills to learn. Oh, and since you'll be graduating next year, don't forget to take the ACT before the end of this school year."

"Okay," I said, though I didn't know what the ACT was. "Why do I need to take it?"

"You'll need it to apply to colleges," he explained. "You're going to college, right?"

"I think so," I answered spontaneously. In truth, I hadn't

considered the possibility of attending college. If I did go to college, I would be the first in my immediate family to do so.

"Well, I think you should go."

"Thank you," I responded. We shook hands, and I walked out of Mr. Dernbach's office amazed and excited to be graduating early.

I followed through with Mr. Dernbach's advice and took the ACT test that spring. However, I did so reluctantly, because I worried that a low score would prove I was stupid. Near the end of the school year, we got our ACT scores. Some students gloated, while some of us simply kept quiet. I remained silent because I had no idea what the scores meant in the context of my life or future. Nevertheless, I also followed through with Mr. Dernbach's advice to apply to college. I applied to DeVry Institute of Technology in Lombard, Illinois, because I wanted to study telecommunications, and UW–Green Bay because it was close to home.

I also signed up for a job training program for the summer. Before school ended, I learned I was assigned to Green Bay East High School, where I would clean bathrooms, desks, floors, and other parts of the building. It seemed as though my summer would be spent cleaning, spending time with Duene, and playing soccer. Before the end of the school year, I received a letter out of the blue.

> Dear Pao,
> Congratulations! Because of your all-conference selection, we would like to invite you to try out for a team that will travel to play in several soccer tournaments in Europe in August. Please see the location and time below.
>
> Date: Saturday, May 21, 1988
> Location: Coburn Park
> Time: 10 a.m.
>
> Please wear proper soccer cleats, socks, and shin guards.
> We look forward to seeing you there.

I couldn't find Europe on a map, but I was excited to have been invited and eagerly looked forward to the tryouts. I didn't know anyone there, but I felt confident during the drills and scrimmages. A few weeks later, a letter informed me that I made the team. I was thrilled until I looked at the cost—over two thousand dollars. Though the letter included materials to help raise the money, I knew I could never sell enough candies and pizzas to raise two thousand dollars. As badly as I wanted to go, I didn't even bother asking Vue. I was willing to ask for a hundred dollars for driver's ed, but I knew we couldn't spare two thousand dollars just for me to play soccer.

Not long after this disappointment, I received more bad news. Duene called one evening in late June, after I had just arrived home from a hard day of work and soccer practice. I was so glad she had called. "How's your day?" I began, but then I heard her sobbing.

"Pao," she said, "I have something to tell you."

The previous month, after I'd gotten comfortable driving the Escort, I'd visited her home in Berlin and met her family. They invited me to spend the night, so I stayed and slept on their sofa. The next morning, Duene woke up early and crept downstairs to wake me so we could snuggle on the sofa before I left. I left before the rest of her family was up. On my way home, I thought about how her willingness to take such a risk showed how much she loved me. I knew I loved her, too.

"Pao," she said through tears. "I've been arranged to marry my cousin from California. He is the son of my mom's sister." I had been hardened by almost ten years as an orphan, but deep down, I could feel my heart breaking. I didn't want to believe it. I was infuriated—not just because she was a seventeen-year-old being forced into an arranged marriage, but also because her cousin and future husband was in his late twenties. I'd just gotten my driver's license a few months ago, and this man was almost twice my age.

"When are they coming?" I asked, trying hard to remain calm.

"Next weekend. They're flying in."

"That's in a week." I was in disbelief.

"Yes," she said. "Can you do me a favor?"

"Yes, of course."

"Can you stop by tomorrow?"

"Are you sure?" I asked. "What about your family?"

"Don't worry. They will all be working. I'll be home alone. Get here around ten. Okay?"

"Yes, I will be there."

All of a sudden, her voice changed to a whisper. "Sorry, I can't talk anymore. My mom is coming."

"Okay," I said. "I'll see you tomorrow."

Lying awake in bed that night, I pondered why she wanted to see me. Maybe she wanted to elope with me. Maybe we would run away like other Hmong couples I had heard about or couples I had seen in romantic Indian and Chinese movies. But then reality hit me. How would I support her? I was just a high school sophomore. I'd only been driving for a few months, and my job cleaning East High barely covered my gas.

My drive to Berlin the next morning was long. When I arrived, Duene led me upstairs. We sat on a balcony overlooking a few warehouses and some train tracks in the distance.

"I asked you to come because I wanted to see you for the last time," she said. "And I wanted to return all your gifts. I don't want to take them with me to remind me of you, but I didn't want to throw them away. It wouldn't be fair to you."

I didn't know what to say. She handed me the gifts I'd given her, including the cheap broken-heart necklace from Christmas. She cried and cried, but I didn't. I knew I just didn't have the emotional bandwidth to do what I had considered earlier and take her home with me.

We hugged for a long, long time. Then I left.

It was a long drive home from Berlin. I was so dazed, I almost rear-ended a semitruck on the highway. After I got home, I put all her letters and gifts inside a box and stored it in my closet. I continued to wear the sweater she gave me until it was worn out. All summer, I thought of her and missed her dearly. But I never saw her again.

What kept me sane was soccer. I'd been invited to play with a U-19 team sponsored by Bank One along with a few players I had competed against in high school. I played in my usual position as a central midfielder. I loved our uniform—a bright red, striped top with white shorts and socks—and I loved playing for my coach, Horst Stemke. He was my first soccer coach who was white. I loved his calm demeanor. The games and practices allowed me to escape the sadness and hard work that filled the rest of my days.

Life didn't get any easier for me as summer progressed. After my job training at the high school ended, I got a job as a dishwasher at the Petite Stein in downtown Green Bay. The water was unbelievably hot. I'd worn gloves during my custodial work at East but I didn't as a dishwasher. It often felt like my hands were on fire. Also, I was lonely and still getting over Duene. I started to believe nothing in life comes easy—at least, not for anyone as unprivileged as me.

One day, the owner of the Petite Stein offered me the opportunity to clean the bar on Saturday and Sunday mornings. At first, I said no, since my weekends were already so busy. But he convinced me when he said, "Anything you find is yours, including money."

After several weekends of cleaning, I realized there was no money or anything valuable to be found, so I told the owner I wanted to stick to dishwashing. About a week later, he promoted me to busing, which was easier than dishwashing. But the waitresses turned me off. They watched me like a hawk, thinking I was going to steal their tips.

Finally, I caught a break. A few weeks after school started, Vue told me a lady had called and left a message for me to call her back. When I called back the next day, I spoke with a woman from Job Service. A few weeks earlier, I had visited Job Service and submitted an application. The woman told me she had the perfect job lined up for me.

"It's working for a law firm," she said, "and you can start right away. I already told them you're the perfect person for the job."

"Really?" I was immediately excited about the opportunity.

I called the employer and set up an interview for the next day. The Grzeca and Stanton law firm was on Riverside Drive along the Fox River in Allouez. When I arrived, I met with Marie and Mike, the owners of the firm. After a few questions, they wanted to know how soon I could start. I thought about my current situation at the restaurant and said, "Immediately."

I began working at the firm for an hour or so every day between school and soccer. I got paid $3.35 per hour. I operated the Xerox machine, making copies of depositions, and I also organized files and delivered documents to other firms and courthouses around the area. Mark, one of the attorneys, drove a slick, jet-black Chevrolet Beretta. With his immaculate hair, he reminded me of a character from a television show. Sandy, another attorney, was elegant and sophisticated. Mike's wife, Linda, was the office secretary. One day, she invited me to speak about the Hmong experience to her daughter's fifth grade class in Denmark, Wisconsin. It was my first time presenting in front of a large crowd, and I really enjoyed it.

Working at the law firm broadened my horizons. I discovered lives and careers beyond my experience, and these new and emerging possibilities began to change the trajectory of my life.

6

We scored. They scored. They scored. We scored. The game ended two–two. We went into overtime—two ten-minute halves with the "golden goal" rule. If they score first, they win. If we score first, we win.

We kicked off. Like every kickoff we'd had for the last two seasons, our forward Dan tapped me the ball. Our teammates knew what to expect next. In these scenarios, I would usually gather the ball, turn around to face our midfielders, and pass the ball to one of them. But on this kickoff, I gathered the ball, turned to my midfielders, and held onto the ball. I noticed the opposing team's two forwards didn't force me to make the backward pass. Instead, they were rushing toward our midfielders.

I instinctively pulled the ball back to face the opponents' goal. To my surprise, their two central midfielders sagged into a defensive position. That meant I now had about twenty yards of open space before anyone could defend me, which had never happened before. Usually, several defenders were always right on me.

With that opening, I made my move. As I started dribbling the ball toward the goal, I noticed in my peripheral vision that nobody was reacting. I figured if I was fast enough, I could dribble straight to the goal with only five players to beat: their two central midfielders, stopper, sweeper, and goalie.

When the two central midfielders noticed me coming, they panicked and rushed toward me. At the last second, I tapped the ball between them and passed them with a quick burst of speed. They didn't even touch me.

Seeing that, the stopper also panicked and rushed to defend

This photo of the 1988 All-Metro Soccer Team was published in the *Green Bay News-Chronicle*. I am kneeling in the center of the front row. Though I didn't realize it at the time, it was quite an achievement to have been named the best player in my position and one of the best eleven high school soccer players in the area.

me. I dribbled right at him and, again at the last second, made a sharp forty-five degree cut and sailed by. After the sweeper made the same strategic error, I had only the goalie left. I dribbled to his left and tucked the ball into the right corner of the net.

Before I realized it, all of my teammates, both on and off the field, were running toward me. They piled on me, shouting, and we all went crazy. It was one of the few euphoric moments of my life thus far.

As usual, none of my family members were there to celebrate the moment with me, but I thought nothing of it. After the game, I got into my brother-in-law's Corolla, drove out of the park, and took a right onto Libal Street. The appropriately titled "Fortunate Son" by Creedence Clearwater Revival was playing on the radio. I smiled the whole way home.

A few weeks later, I learned I made the all-conference team and all-metro team for the second year in a row. I was one of three players who had also received those honors the year before.

November brought more good luck as I received acceptance letters from both DeVry Institute of Technology and UW–Green Bay. I was thrilled. I completed the required paperwork to attend DeVry and submitted a hundred-dollar housing deposit. A representative even visited me. But then, after much discussion with Vue, my older sister Yanghoua, and my brother-in-law, I decided to attend Green Bay to be closer to home. The turning point came when my sister asked, "What if you got sick and needed help? Who would be there for you?" I was very independent, but I wasn't ready to leave the support of my family.

I was especially relieved to get my college acceptance letters because I was still figuring out how to be a student. In my fall semester at East, I enjoyed my two language arts classes. In composition, we watched movies in class and then wrote papers about topics related to the movies. Many of my classmates simply slept through class, but I loved watching the movies, and I loved the academic freedom even more. I also loved our teacher, Ms. Frederick. She provided feedback on my papers without covering them in red ink, adding a few comments here and there about my grammar and always complimenting the content.

My American literature class with Mrs. Smith was very different but also enjoyable. She gave us a spelling list every Monday and then a test every Friday. She assigned stories for us to read and gave points to those who responded to questions about the stories in class. I hated speaking in class, but I wanted to get a good grade. So, I voraciously read the assigned stories and made certain I could answer the questions she would ask. At the end of the semester, I earned an A in Mrs. Smith's class, a grade I had heard she rarely gave out. I felt I achieved something.

Plus, due to my work ethic and behavior, I sensed Mrs. Smith respected me.

But my grades in some other classes weren't as good. I was distraught when I learned I got a C+ in chemistry. I gave that class everything I had, and I was two tenths of a percentage away from getting a B-. But my strict teacher wasn't about to change it. Along with my poor grade in biology from the previous year, the C+ simply compounded my distaste for the sciences.

I struggled mightily in trigonometry as well. The combination of mathematic equations and reading comprehension did me in. I could figure out the equations but not the story problems. It also didn't help that I sat right behind a freshman who was a mathematical genius. Every day, I watched him fiddling and doodling, not paying any attention to the teacher, but when he got his test scores back, he aced almost every one. Keith, a senior and friend who sat next me, struggled even more than me. We ended our misery by dropping the course. But I had to keep my chemistry class.

In early December, I found myself at my uncle's house on Maple Street for our annual Hmong New Year ritual. Unlike some other Hmong children of my age, I didn't grow up attending many Hmong rituals, traditions, or shamanistic ceremonies. Still, I knew we performed the ancient Hmong New Year ritual to welcome the New Year, to ask for good blessings, and to send away all the bad karma and evil spirits from the previous year. Amid the highways, Christmas lights, churches, Green Bay Packers' gear, and wintry blizzards, we did our best to continue our Hmong traditions. Within the confines of our tiny rented apartments and duplexes, many Hmong families like mine burned incense, set altars to the spirits and ancestors, conducted soul-calling rituals and shamanistic ceremonies, and sacrificed chickens, pigs, cows, and sometimes even goats.

Some believed that failure to attend the rituals had negative consequences, like being punished or disowned by the ancestors or being captured and held hostage by evil spirits, which could lead to illness or death. But even in the face of such high stakes, I avoided many of the rituals and ceremonies that my other relatives attended. When I did reluctantly attend, I never paid much attention. I simply wasn't comfortable in those spaces.

Yet, I'd decided to attend the New Year ritual at my uncle's because, deep down, I still had a strong sense of cultural obligation. Midway into the proceedings, I knew from some similar events I'd attended in the past that it was time for me to drink a shot of hard liquor. Supposedly, the shot contained good blessings from the elders, spirits, and ancestors. Having drunk it a few times before, I knew I hated its smell and the scorching sensation it sent cascading down my esophagus. The feeling of it settling at the bottom of my empty stomach was worst of all. But I drank it anyway.

I looked forward to eating the fresh boiled chicken with tofu and rice, but this required patience. Before we could eat, my uncle had to perform a ritual to the good spirits that had protected us last year and would protect us in the coming year. He set up a small round table and a chair in the corner of the kitchen. He then filled a bowl with boiled chicken and tofu and a plate with rice and centered them on the table. He grabbed many spoons and arranged them face down around the edges of the bowl and plate, keeping one spoon in his hand. Then he began mumbling phrases in Hmong that I had never heard before and didn't understand. He took a spoonful of rice and placed it on the table, then he took a spoonful of broth from the bowl of chicken and tofu and poured it over the rice. Finally, he used his hands to shred some small pieces of chicken and added those to the rice and broth.

As my uncle repeated this process, he began mumbling louder.

When I heard my father's name, that got my attention, and I tuned in. But after about a minute, when I still couldn't understand the words that sounded like gibberish to me, I disengaged. I was very glad when we finally got to eat.

Some weeks after the New Year ceremony, I had the chance to ask my uncle why he had mentioned my father's name during the ritual. He explained, "Since your father passed away many years ago and because he is now one of our ancestors, I was inviting him, along with the other ancestors and the other good spirits of the world, to come and join us for the meal. I asked them to protect the family from harm and evil spirits in the year to come. Typically, we try to include at least three or four generations of ancestors."

Wow that's interesting! I thought. He went on to tell me more information with a great sense of importance, but it simply went in one ear and out the other. My disengagement was a sign that I was losing interest in these ancestral traditions.

Later that December, I attended the Hmong New Year at the Armory in Sheboygan. While waiting for some friends, cousins, and uncles to arrive, I listened to some traditional chanting, or kwv txhiaj, which is one of our ancient ways of passing on stories about love, tragedy, ethics, morals, and other life lessons to the next generation.

One chant was about us leaving our native homeland of Laos. The words addressed the sorrow that filled our hearts and spirits, the challenges that we now face and will face in the future, and how we must try to reestablish our cultural legitimacy in our new world. Most of the metaphors eluded me, but these lyrics resonated with me.

> The orphan way of life,
> I hadn't wished for me.

I hadn't dreamed of it.
But it came for me.

I would never wish it upon you.
I would never dream it upon you.
For it is harsh.
For it is unforgiving.

My parents didn't want to die.
But the evil ways came and got them.
My parents didn't want to die.
But the evil ways took them away.

I've often moaned in pain and in sorrow.
A butterfly builds its cocoon but I've no home.
Whereas a butterfly is beautiful, I dress in rags.
Where a butterfly has comfort, I don't.

The evil ways, the evil ways have taken away my nourishment.

Being an orphan is like being a rice field.
If the owners don't add water, there's no life.
If the owners don't add water, there's no sweetness to the rice.
If the owners don't add water, there's no nourishment.

When I'm sick, people say I'm lazy.
When I'm in good health, people say I eat too much.
I don't get new clothes.
I only get leftovers.

Where are my parents?
Come, come my parents, and comfort me.
Come, come my parents, and comfort all the orphans.

Heal me when I'm sick.
Feed me when I'm hungry.
Dress me.

The evil ways, the evil ways have taken away my nourishment.

The words struck me as depressing and true. Being an orphan made me feel like a dark shadow had been cast over me. People in my life had the power to either make that shadow vanish or intensify it. But I was beginning to realize that I, too, had the power to change that narrative.

After the chanting on the stage ended, I joined a few friends, cousins, and uncles who had arrived and were now sitting in metal chairs in the audience. The party was now in full swing as people came and went, conversing and dancing on the floor in front of the stage. When a slow song came on, I approached a girl and asked for a dance. She had on a slick, tight black dress and was wearing an abundance of make-up, hair spray, and perfume—things the elders had advised me to avoid when courting a potential spouse.

As we danced, I felt mesmerized by her beauty, but I very much valued authenticity. During my slow dance with Maya two years earlier, I had appreciated her openness and lack of vanity. Though I may not have fully realized it yet, Maya had become my benchmark for who was truly authentic. I danced with the girl a few more times and learned she was seventeen and lived in Sheboygan. I usually gravitated toward girls a bit older than me, which is quite contrary to Hmong courting norms. In fact, for some, it's a cultural taboo.

Finally, I told my cousins, uncles, and friends that I was leaving. I had come alone, and I would leave alone. On other nights, I had waited to give some friends or relatives a ride home. But that night, with weighty thoughts of love, relationships, and family on my mind, I craved the freedom of time alone in my car.

Feeling invincible, I coasted along the dark strip of Highway 43, going seventy and sometimes eighty miles per hour in Vue's Ford Escort. My AM radio was picking up songs from the fifties, sixties, and seventies, and I turned the volume up high.

When I passed Two Rivers, I knew I was about thirty minutes from home. I momentarily took my eyes off the road to adjust the radio, and when I looked up, a deer was in front of me. Then, everything went black.

When I regained consciousness, I felt dazed. I had no idea how much time had passed, but I couldn't ignore two distinctive odors. One was radiator coolant and the other was the deer.

I released my seat belt and stepped out onto the gravel shoulder of the highway. The car had stopped just a few feet short of plunging down an embankment. The Escort's hood was now a crater—the headlights crushed, the grill smashed, the bumper bent, and the radiator torn and leaking. Deer hair and blood covered everything. But I didn't see any deer.

How am I going to talk to Vue about this? I worried. *Is he going to yell at me? Is he going to take the car away from me? Who's going to fix it? Do we even have the money?* But these were questions for the future. In the moment, I had no idea where I was. It was silent, and there was no light in sight.

Then, I saw a car approaching from the same direction I had been traveling. "Please stop. Please stop. Please stop," I whispered. But the car zoomed by. I ran behind it, hoping it would stop and return. Then the brake lights came on. The car stopped and began backing up. I soon recognized it—a brown Corolla that belonged to an uncle who had also been at the party. When my uncle and the other passengers got out, they looked worried.

"Pao! You okay, man?" they asked.

"Yeah, I'm all right," I replied, not really knowing if I was indeed okay.

"Whoa, that's some damage," someone said. "So glad you're all right. What happened?"

I told them, then got in the back seat of the Corolla. The ride home felt very long. At my house, everyone watched as I took my time getting to the door. I knocked instead of using my key. Vue came, and I waved to my uncle and everybody else. Once inside, I reluctantly and chokingly told Vue what had happened.

"As long as you're okay, don't worry about the car," he said. "Go to bed. We'll go and get it tomorrow." I was incredibly grateful for his caring, nonthreatening response. But as I lay in bed, I still felt very unsettled. I wished that when I woke up later, I would go downstairs, look out our kitchen window, and see the car in the driveway, as though nothing had happened. After a while, I closed my eyes and floated off into sleep.

Sadly, that wish did not come true. When Vue woke up, I was grateful all over again that he didn't chide me. I'd worried that he was just too tired to let out his frustration and disappointment the night before. He called the Green Bay police and asked them for the phone number of the Two Rivers police department. He then called the Two Rivers police department, and the officer there gave us the phone number of a local tow business near where the accident likely occurred. Vue then called the tow place and told them to meet us at the site.

The dried streak of blood on the pavement stretched for about fifty yards. A huge deer was lying on the opposite shoulder of the highway about one hundred yards from my car. The truck driver towed the car back to our house. Since we didn't have insurance coverage, Vue and I decided to fix it ourselves. We bought a new headlight and radiator, and we straightened out the hood so it would latch again. After a few weeks, I felt comfortable driving to school, work, and various social events, but I avoided night driving on the highway at all costs.

If my parents had been alive, they would have done a hus plig—a soul-calling ceremony—or even a shamanistic ritual. Many Hmong still rely on such ceremonies to reunite their wandering souls with their physical beings. Vue had recently converted to Christianity, and I was pretty sure he prayed for me. I remembered what Vang, my eldest brother, once told me as we fished together on the Manitowoc River: "Pao, don't worry. Wherever you go, I'm always protecting you and our siblings. So, don't worry. I'm with you. My spirits are always with you and protecting you." But I wasn't sure what I believed.

Having received no cultural indoctrination, I thought that if one of my souls were to ever leave or reject my physical being, I would just go after it myself, catch it, and put it right back into my physical being again. And if I learned that the devil had taken it, I would go to hell, barter with the devil, and if need be, fight the devil to get it back.

In April, I was surprised to learn that I could register for classes at UW–Green Bay early due to my academic achievement. I ranked 32 out of 332 students in my grade, meaning I was in the top 10 percent. I considered myself an average student. After all, my GPA was barely above a 3.3. I had my graduating class to thank.

I drove to campus by myself for registration. I joined a group of other incoming first-year students. First, we sat around a table in the Student Union and had a brief "get to know you" session. I hadn't done anything like that before, not even in high school, and due to my introverted nature, I disliked it. I just wanted to get down to business and be on my way home. I did share with my group that I would like to try out for the university's soccer team.

An adviser then shared information with us that I found completely confusing—general education courses, majors, minors, interdisciplinary studies, electives, housing options, and many other things. I felt completely overwhelmed but enrolled in French, psychology, algebra and trigonometry, and an expository writing class. I drove home feeling certain that every student on campus was smarter than me.

Since graduating students did not need to attend the last week of high school classes, I asked Mrs. Smith if I could take my final exam early. She was surprised I was graduating, since I was a junior. She accommodated my request and even congratulated me with a huge smile. I believe I was one of just a few students who experienced that side of her. On my last day in her class, I finally shared the news of my graduation with my classmates. They all expressed surprise and excitement. Many of us had been together since eighth grade. I didn't realize I would never see most of them again.

Speech was my last high school class. I had signed up for the class hoping to end my fear of public speaking. But as I prepared to give my last speech, I felt as if I was about to have a heart attack before my turn, just as I had before my prior four speeches. My heart pumped so fast, I felt it would burst out of my chest, and my blood seemed to boil in my veins. As I approached the podium, I thought my legs might give out and cause me to collapse. Fortunately, none of that happened.

For some unknown reason, I had chosen the topic of how to build a fence for goats on a farm. I had no knowledge of goats or how to build a fence. I planned to give a demonstration using Popsicle sticks, glue, and a few plastic goat figurines. My three-minute speech ended up being almost ten minutes long. At some point, I stopped following my notecards and started talking about how I would make an electric fence and build a moat and bridges. When I received my grade, I was surprised my teacher didn't take off many points. He must have been glad to see a quiet and reserved student finally having some fun in front of the class.

Before graduation, a few friends, cousins, and I decided to take a road trip to Chicago. It was our first time heading to a big city without adults. Even though it was mid-May, it was snowing when we left Green Bay. But it was sunny by the time we got to Chicago. Seeing Chicago up close, especially the skyscrapers and busy traffic, reminded me of when my siblings and I stopped in

A few weeks before my graduation from Green Bay High School in 1989, I asked my brother Kong to take some photos of me in my Michael Jackson jacket. It was a side of me that I did not share with most people.

Hong Kong on our journey from Thailand to the United States. As a seven-year-old, I had been mesmerized by that big city, but I felt comfortable and even inspired as I explored Chicago. We visited Chinatown and Little Vietnam. We then visited the Sears Tower. I had such a fear of heights that I could barely walk as we looked down over Chicago.

A few days later, as I sat through my graduation ceremony at the Brown County Arena, I thought of the words I'd heard from many local Hmong elders. "High school graduates," they would scoff. "They can't write or interpret. They can't even spell or write a check." I was the fifth or sixth class of Hmong teenagers to graduate from high school in Green Bay, and in the eyes of these elders, we had all been disappointing. Our elders had high expectations. They expected a great deal from us given what they sacrificed to give us the opportunity of living in the United States. Their words were hurtful. But at the same time, I understood that the elders lacked context. They didn't understand the unique psychological and cultural struggles plaguing my generation. Learning English and figuring out how to be successful in our new world wasn't always our priority. Our priority was often psychological and physical safety.

Many of my family members attended the ceremony, and Vue took some pictures. I walked out of the Brown County Arena not knowing if I would be the same as the Hmong high school graduates who had preceded me.

In the ensuing months, parents of my fellow Hmong high school graduates did as much as they could to give their graduates a fighting chance, holding many celebrations and blessing events. Elders, leaders, family members, community members, and special guests were invited to bless these graduates so that they would have a successful future. I didn't have parents to organize a celebration for me. And I knew a celebration wouldn't help me nearly as much as my own motivation, abilities, high expectations, and a bit of luck.

I still had a lingering belief that I was culturally and intellectually inferior to most of my peers. And I didn't know what to expect from my future. But when fall arrived, I would be a student at the University of Wisconsin–Green Bay—a new mystery awaiting me.

PART II

The Abyss

Something deep in my character allows me to take the hits and get on with trying to win.

—Lionel Messi

7

I arrived on the UW–Green Bay campus early for my first day of college. The morning was cold and windy. I felt excited, but also very nervous and uncertain. Vue and Yanghoua were there to drop me off. For more than ten years now, Vue had been a father figure to me, and Yanghoua had been a mother figure, even though she had been in California for much of that time. She and her family had recently moved back to Green Bay and were living in the apartment below us on South Webster Avenue. A few weeks earlier, I had left my job at Grzeca and Stanton and referred one of my uncles as my replacement. I was lucky to have received a grant that would cover nearly all of my college expenses, including tuition and housing. Now, my job would be focusing on my education.

I had been assigned to live in Ted Lenfestey Hall, one of the residence halls closest to some of the more recently constructed buildings on campus, including the Student Union. My roommate wouldn't arrive until later that evening. He had sent me a letter a couple weeks earlier. Our room on the second floor had a bunk bed, two study desks, two five-drawer dressers, and a small bathroom. This was a relief. I knew from my precollege experience at UW–Oshkosh that I didn't like communal bathrooms. For bedding, I had brought two pillows, two bed sheets, and two blankets. In my luggage, I had five pairs of pants, eight pairs of underwear, ten pairs of socks, ten button-down shirts, and a couple of T-shirts. I was particular about what I needed to pack and wasn't a fan of T-shirts. In case I missed home, Yanghoua had packed me a box with thirty packets of instant Kung Fu Noodles, a bag of rice, and an electric rice cooker.

I felt a sense of freedom as I watched my siblings drive away in Yanghoua's gigantic Jeep Grand Cherokee. Thankfully, Vue allowed me to keep the Ford Escort on campus. For the second year in a row, I was playing on a U-19 competitive soccer team, and I needed to attend practices, games, and tournaments. I also wanted to attend local and out-of-town parties and other social and cultural events. More importantly, I wanted to visit Maya when she was home in Kimberly or at UW–Oshkosh where she was starting her second year as a student. Over the past year, I'd had the good fortune of running into her a few times at parties and soccer tournaments. Though our meetings had been brief, I had grown very fond of Maya, and I wanted to be more intentional about spending time with her.

As I waited for my roommate to arrive, I roamed the tranquil campus and then the arboretum trail. The environment was scenic and serene, but I was unsettled by the lack of restaurants, stores, and houses around me. The trees and thick bushes along the trail reminded me of where I grew up in Laos and Thailand. As I walked, I couldn't stop existential questions from invading my mind. *Who am I? Why am I here? What if I don't make it out of college? How will I tell my family and friends if I fail? And if I don't make it, what other options do I have?* I was relieved when my dorm finally came back into sight.

I survived the first several weeks of classes, and by November, my college life had become routine. I had picked up a part-time job at the Rathskeller, a pub in the Student Union basement, to cover basic expenses like gas, food, and entertainment. I found listening to lectures, taking notes, completing assignments, and taking quizzes and exams demanding but manageable. However, I was demoralized by a few poor quiz scores, which brought back memories of my struggles in high school biology and chemistry. Always lurking in the background was my sense of inferiority.

And I had no plan in place in the event of failure, which horrified me even more. To ease my mind, I tried to compare my college experience to my life experience over the last decade. I just needed to persevere, make steady progress, and accept that I would inevitably make mistakes and fail—sometimes miserably.

Life with my roommate had also become routine but not in a good way. Shane was tall and lanky, and when he walked, he reminded me of a sloth. I was annoyed by the way he kept his two small fans running all day and all night. I was sensitive to the fan noise and hadn't been sleeping well, and by November, the cool breeze from the fans exacerbated the already-cold weather. Adding to my misery, he also kept our windows open.

It felt to me as though Shane had taken over our room. He had been staying up late and increasing his drinking, and he hadn't been attending classes since October. He no longer dined in the union, and I had no idea what he consumed other than his favorite drink, hard liquor mixed with Coke—a mixture that was completely unfamiliar to me. In order to escape this toxic situation, I stayed late in the computer lab, picked up more working hours at the Rathskeller. And most weekends, I either visited my family or spent time with Maya. While Maya and I weren't in an official relationship, we hung out and enjoyed each other's company whenever we could find time.

One Tuesday night, I had an upsetting experience. I wasn't scheduled to work, so I decided to pull an all-nighter in the computer lab to escape my awful dorm room. I worked on my course assignments, and when I needed a break, I wrote love letters and poems to Maya—though I never intended to share them with her. When I got tired, I closed my eyes and floated into deep space. I thought about the stars, the planets, and the universe. Then I would turn my attention back to my work.

I repeated this process many times. But suddenly, my peaceful thoughts were interrupted by a kaleidoscope of snapshots from my past. *The opium fields. My father. My mother. Explosions. Darkness. The endless walking. Flares. Ants. Dead people. The terrible smell. The brown serpent.* A recurring vision from my childhood—a huge, grotesque, purple tongue emerging from a dead person's mouth—snapped me back to reality. Terrified, I grabbed my stuff and left for my dorm.

I hated going through the underground tunnels on campus, especially late at night. I was certain evil spirits inhabited those spaces at that time of day, yet I had no idea why I was so certain. Maybe it was just my imagination playing tricks on me. I rushed through the tunnel that led to my dorm and breathed in the cool night on the other side. But then I became unsettled again. I sensed that I was being watched by the spirits of the land, which had both good and bad intentions. Not far from my dorm, my body tensed up. Soon, blood was boiling through my veins and tears flooded from my eyes, cascading down my cheeks.

The more I tried to resist the bombardment of memories, the more they intensified. I couldn't control it. Overwhelmed, I sat down on the cold grass and curled forward into a ball. My past had caught up to me, and I didn't know how to deal with it.

Later, after I made it to my room and crawled into bed, I thought about how I could begin to heal my disturbed mind. I was determined to find a way that wasn't religious or spiritual, because I wasn't a part of those worlds. But one way or another, I had healing to do.

Almost all of my time was now spent away from my dorm and my roommate. During the day after classes, I hung out with my Hmong friends, who lived in the residence hall across from mine. They were from Milwaukee and had come to UW–Green Bay because of the contrasting environment—the university was located outside the city, nestled between Lake Michigan, farmland, and emerging subdivisions.

After my friends and I started the Hmong Student Association at UW–Green Bay in 1989, I spent time in the Intercultural American Center with students from the Black Student Union and Native American Student Association, among others. I am sitting at far left in a white turtleneck.

In between classes, I found safety and comfort going to the Intercultural American Center, located on the ground floor of the Colfrin Library. The large windows made it a very pleasant space. There, I was among students who were Native, Asian American, and African American, along with a few international students. I felt safe to discuss and debate politics, academics, and issues of culture, race, and ethnicity. It greatly helped that Deb Moutry, a Black woman, was our adviser. The center was one of the few places where I came across non-white faculty and staff.

Some other Hmong students and I had started a Hmong Student Association earlier in the fall semester, and I was elected vice president. I enjoyed attending the meetings and activities and sometimes, in the absence of our president, even university meetings. The other Hmong students in the group were older than me, and I respected them as my older brothers and sisters.

A few were married with children. One Hmong student who had recently moved from California knew Mee, who had been my second-grade girlfriend. He showed me a picture of her, and I couldn't believe how she had grown up to be a beautiful young woman. Even though Hmong refugees were spread out across the country, all of our familial and cultural connections sometimes made it feel like a very small community.

On the weekends, I either went home to visit friends and play indoor soccer or I drove to Oshkosh to visit Maya. There, she and I went to the movies, hung out at the park, spent time in her room, and ate out. We ordered chicken lad na at the Mekong River Restaurant; French dip sandwiches at Heroes, a local pub; and hot wings at Kentucky Fried Chicken. This was the beginning of my culinary journey. Sometimes after catching a late movie, we would sleep in my car in the parking lot of the cinema; otherwise, I would have to drop her off at her dorm, which meant I would need to head home because of her roommate.

Being with Maya, I experienced extraordinary inner peace. I felt wanted, needed, and appreciated. I even discovered that hidden deep inside myself, I had a sense of humor. I felt as though time was jealous of our joy because every second, minute, hour, and day passed more quickly as our relationship progressed and transformed.

My time with Maya made me truly hate returning to my dorm. It wasn't until the last week of classes that I finally reached a breaking point. Coming inside from the cold December day, I became completely deflated when I saw Shane's two fans running and our window open. The thermostat read fifty-six degrees. I'm sure my resident advisor had told us what to do in a situation like this, but whatever I had been told, addressing interpersonal conflicts simply wasn't my forte.

The semester finally ended, and the holiday break saved me. My roommate left to join his family in Michigan. I was glad that something good was still within him. I was also thankful for an important lesson I had learned before everything soured between us. A week or so after classes started, he and I compared papers we had written for our expository writing class. Mine was marked for grammatical errors while his was marked for content and academic language. I had previously assumed that my white classmates did not receive any marks on their writing papers, but I was wrong. It was a small but profound moment that lessened my sense of intellectual inferiority.

In January, I received my first semester grades. My grade point average was above 3.0, but I received a BC in algebra and trigonometry, a four-credit course. This didn't surprise me, but it demoralized me. Yes, I was lost most of the time in class as the robotic professor demonstrated various math scenarios on the board, but I had attended every lecture, taken detailed notes, and gone to every class discussion. I didn't know what else I could have done to improve my grade or how to improve moving forward. My self-esteem further plummeted when I learned that a Hmong classmate had earned an AB in the same course, and he had been in the US for just a few years. Since I had lived in the US for longer, I assumed I would get a better grade than him, but I now saw that this was a flawed assumption.

I took a three-week course in human biology during the January interim session. It was a typical course, except the professor gave us the option to challenge—in writing—any test questions that we got wrong. I enjoyed challenging most of the questions I got wrong. However, all of that work returned minimal academic dividends, and I didn't do well in the course.

The one bright side of the January session was that I commuted every day to campus. I had packed up all of my belongings before leaving for winter break. I would not be returning to my dorm room for the spring semester.

8

For the spring semester of 1990, I continued to commute to campus, relieved to be away from my room and my roommate. I desperately needed peace to minimize both my academic and psychological deterioration. If I dropped out of college, it would feel like I was letting my demons take control of my well-being. Also, if I dropped out, I had no Plan B. I would be in misery, and I wanted to avoid that.

I was living with my family at 519 Third Street, in a place Vue had purchased earlier in the year. The house looked like a barn, with two floors and a small, creepy basement. One night, Kong and I heard something fluttering in the ceiling and then throughout the house. We were frightened and gathered in the living room. Soon we saw a bat flying between the dining room, kitchen, half bath, and living room. I grabbed a blanket and my nunchunks. With the blanket wrapped around me from my head to my feet, I stood in the middle of the living room waiting for the bat. When it flew near me, I whacked it with my nunchunks. I then grabbed a pair of gloves, picked it up, and threw it in the trash can. We couldn't sleep after that, so Kong and I played Shinobi on our Sega system until dawn.

After leaving my campus living situation, I'd quit my job at the Rathskeller and picked up a new position in receiving at Sears. On most days, I drove the Escort. Since we'd repaired it ourselves, it was difficult to close the hood properly. When it was sunny, I borrowed Pheng's 1978 white T-Top Trans Am. It was terrible on gas, but I loved driving it, as it reminded me of the car Burt Reynolds drove in *Smokey and the Bandit*.

Once my classes were over for the day, I was free to visit places that helped heal and nurture my well-being, like Bay Shore County Park, Point Comfort, and Bay Beach, among other scenic sites. I could now eat at various restaurants and hang out with friends outside of the university. My job at Sears gave me money to support my basic needs and to visit Maya on the weekends or sometimes during the week when my soccer team had a game nearby. I loved visiting her after a game. We would walk with her nieces and nephews to Sunset Park, and then she would cook me dinner before I headed home.

When I really needed an escape from the world, I returned to my bedroom on Third Street, which was decorated with a few posters of Bruce Lee and sports cars, as well as my artwork from sixth grade. I began spending less time at the Intercultural American Center and saw my university Hmong and non-Hmong friends less frequently. Somehow, that felt like what I needed. I felt so relieved to have escaped the confines of my residence hall and campus life.

In the middle of the semester, I attended some job fairs on campus and submitted a few applications. Not long after, the United Parcel Service interviewed and hired me. The pay was a huge upgrade from my job at Sears, but there was a reason—my shifts started before the sun came up. In fact, my supervisor had to call me because I didn't show up for my very first shift, which started at four in the morning. For the next several months, I unloaded boxes from a semitruck trailer and put them on a sliding panel that rolled the items onto a conveyor belt. I had to unload two semitruck trailers before eight each morning because some deliveries needed to be made before ten o'clock. Sometimes the smallest boxes were the heaviest.

After my shift ended at eight, I would then drive to campus for my eight-thirty class. I was so exhausted that I often fell asleep in class. One day, I talked to the manager about my circumstances, and he gave me the new task of loading the delivery trucks. That relieved some physical pressure off my back, but it didn't help with my lack of sleep. Again, I talked to the manager. This time, he changed my shift to evenings, unloading packages that hadn't been delivered that day. That didn't last long either. The work was just too physically demanding. I could feel my body deteriorating at a pace I had never experienced. It impacted my ability to play soccer. Eventually, I decided to leave the job altogether, and I was thankful that my manager was supportive.

One day, as I walked by the Student Services office before heading home, I noticed a list of students who had made the dean's list. I saw the names of several people I knew. *Perhaps I'm not as bright as I thought*, I reflected. Soon, I was consumed by the belief that I was not college material. I became convinced that I would flunk out—it was just a matter of time.

Since the UPS job hadn't worked out, I needed money. One day, I stopped by Career Services to view various job postings. I applied to become a student researcher in the Sociology Department and got the job. I realized I had one asset that many students on campus did not have: I could speak Hmong relatively well. In my new position, I scheduled appointments with local Hmong families and interviewed them about their fish consumption, which was of interest due to the high levels of PCBs (polychlorinated biphenyls) in the water in the area. First, I had to translate background information about the research—which was written in complex, academic language—from English to Hmong. Then, if a Hmong family agreed to participate in the research, I would meet the head of the household and ask them about their background and fishing experiences and about eating the fish in the area.

I didn't fully understand the purpose of the research, but I enjoyed doing the interviews, as I got to meet and learn a lot about many of the Hmong families living in Green Bay. The only part I didn't like about the job was calling people and asking them if they wanted to participate in the study. For the most part, families were very polite and respectful, even when they declined to participate. But a few people accused me of working for the government and digging up information that could be used against them. I wasn't exactly sure where they were getting those ideas, but that experience taught me about some beliefs in the Hmong community that I hadn't been aware of previously. I stayed with that job until the semester ended. The study was halted for the summer.

For a summer job, I then found a less prestigious but fun position at a local pickle factory putting small cucumbers into glass jars. My sister-in-law worked there, too. She had been there for many years, but I didn't get the job because of her. In fact, I didn't know she was working there until I started the job. I felt weird working alongside her—I was a college student working a summer job to earn gas money, and my sister-in-law, who could barely speak English, was working full-time to support her family. But that aside, it was a fun job because many of my Hmong friends from the community also worked there, as did some of their parents and family members. The work was mundane, but being with my friends made the eight hours enjoyable. At the end of the day, I felt that the sense of belonging was more important than the nature of the job.

When my brother Kong, who was now sixteen, told me he needed a job for the summer, I took him with me and completed an application for him. I had planned to take him home after that, but when I gave the completed application to the receptionist, she looked it over and asked, "Can he start today?"

"Yes," I replied.

After a month, while Kong and many of my friends continued to work on the assembly line, my supervisor started moving me to different stations, including the "spicy line" where I put dried red-hot peppers into the pickle jars. I didn't last very long at that station because I kept sneezing and blowing my nose. She then moved me to the basement where I monitored the conveyor belts with already capped pickle jars. If any of the jars fell off a belt or broke, I would sweep them up and put them in the trash. I felt like I was being promoted, but I dearly missed my friends. So, I asked my supervisor if I could return to the line putting cucumbers into glass jars with my friends. Subconsciously, I knew I wasn't ready to move on from my cultural comfort zone.

One late evening in July, as I relaxed on my bed at the Third Street house, I heard guests arriving. I wondered, *Who could be visiting us this late on a Saturday evening? Probably just Vue's in-laws.* A few minutes later, Vue knocked on my bedroom door and asked me to step out. My brother-in-law ChiaSeng and three of his cousins invited me to sit in a chair at our dining table as they stood across from me. *Not again,* I thought. Several months back, we had a similar meeting to address the fact that I'd clipped ChiaSeng's half brother's bumper at a soccer tournament at Appleton's Memorial Park. When it happened, a spectator told me, "Pao, if this car's owner tells you to fix it, don't. It was already falling off—you barely touched it. There's not even a mark on your car or theirs." But after the meeting, I had to pay for the bumper, which was repaired by a mechanic ChiaSeng knew.

This meeting, however, turned out to be something completely different. One of the cousins placed two small cups of beer on a plate and gave it to me. I wasn't sure what I was supposed to do, but they insisted that I take it. I did, although I had no idea what was going on.

"Dab Pao," one of ChiaSeng's cousins said, referring to me as his brother-in-law, "I want to apologize for taking away your precious time. But, as they say, when troubles hit a family, the ones who are near are far and the ones who are far are like the mists and fog. We have looked far and near and cannot see anyone else. And we have come to your doorstep because we need your service and support. I'm sure you have many more important things on your plate, but we have come to seek your service as the best man for a wedding. My brother has gotten engaged, and his wedding will be next weekend." Then, everyone in the group bowed and kneeled twice.

He was so eloquent and I felt so honored that I wanted to say something similar in return, but nothing came out. So, I just nodded, drank the beer, and returned the cups and plate to them, gesturing that I had accepted their request. I didn't know much about Hmong wedding traditions at the time, but it was customary for the best man to be someone from the groom's generation. The person could be his best friend or a relative but not someone from his clan.

Vue then handed me four plates and eight cups. He told me to put two cups on each plate, fill them with beer, and return them to each of the cousins. If I had known what to say in such a moment, I would have said,

> Thank you for thinking highly of me, and thank you for coming. You came because you still embrace and cherish our relationship. You came because you have not forgotten my clan and me. You came because you thought of brotherhood and community support. I am deeply honored by this gesture and hope that I can fulfill my responsibility to your satisfaction. I'll do my very best, within my ability, to ensure that the wedding goes as smoothly as you hope. Again, I deeply appreciate you thinking so highly of me and asking me to be the best man in this most important event. I am honored and look forward to doing all that I can to make this event successful.

After taking my four plates, one of the cousins said, "Dab Pao, I want to thank you, again. Thank you for putting aside your busy schedule and giving us your service. Should you or your family ever need any assistance or support, perhaps you will not think of us, but if you do, we may not be able to support you with riches or cows or pigs, but I can assure you that we will give you all the manpower that we have available. So, don't think twice about seeking our service. And again, I want to thank you for your support because I know the tasks will not be easy. Thank you." Then they drank their beer, which ended the formality.

One of them confirmed, "We'll pick up you this Friday, shortly after work. We'll do a quick send-off before we head to Stevens Point. We want to get there around six or seven o'clock."

"Sounds good," I replied. "Thank you." We shook hands, and they departed. I didn't know what I had gotten myself into, but I understood it was a family obligation. Growing up Hmong, there are certain traditions that you simply immerse yourself in and learn by doing. I would have to cancel my plans to visit Maya.

Friday came, and as they had explained, ChiaSeng and his cousins picked me up and brought me to their house on Western Avenue. Our in-laws may have been the first Hmong family to own a house in Green Bay. I had visited the place once, a long time ago when Yanghoua got married. But from my perspective as a teenager, the house didn't seem as big as it had when I was a child. We immediately went to the basement where a meal had been prepared, including a few plates of thinly sliced gingered pork, a few bowls of pork soup with lemongrass, and two bowls of rice. I was directed to my assigned seat. Two wedding negotiators for Ntxua (the groom) and a bridesmaid also had assigned seats. Things proceeded as they had the previous week, except this time, my in-laws thanked the four of us for helping with the wedding. Before leaving, we brought along a rolled-up blanket and a basket filled with salt, pepper, and other items.

A driver, Ntxua, the bridesmaid, two wedding negotiators, ChiaSeng's cousin, ChiaSeng, and I all piled into a conversion van and headed for Stevens Point. We arrived around six that evening.

Before heading to the wedding venue, even though it was late, we stopped at Iverson Park off Highway 10 and followed the tradition of eating a lunch on the way to the bride's home prepared by the groom's family, consisting of rice, two boiled chickens, salt, and black pepper. The bride's family would prepare the lunch for the return journey after the wedding. In the past, Hmong weddings often took place in distant villages, making these packed lunches essential. Once we were situated around a picnic table, one of the wedding negotiators tore up the chickens, unwrapped the rice, and gave everyone plates and utensils. I was glad to have gotten a drumstick.

The wedding ceremony was set to take place in a unit within a large apartment complex. Our group stood outside for about an hour and a half before we were invited in. I didn't know why at the time, but it's customary for the bride's family to do this to test the groom's family's resolve to care for and love their daughter. This tradition also serves to strengthen and bridge family and community ties between the bride and groom, especially when the two families and clans do not know each other well. When we entered, I realized many people were already there, and some were already drinking heavily.

The bridesmaid and bride disappeared into another part of the house while the rest of our group was guided to the living room where a table had been arranged with two chairs on each side. While Ntxua and I sat on the sofa, our wedding negotiators took two of the chairs on one side, and the bride's negotiators took the other two. Soon, all of the negotiators began talking and drinking. The bride's wedding negotiators would often leave the room and return. I assumed they were bringing information to the bride's family, but I didn't know their whereabouts. As I would later learn, the goal of the negotiation is to successfully navigate topics that can sometimes be complicated, such as family history and details related to the dowry. The routine repeated throughout the evening all the way into the early morning, around two or so. Finally, to conclude the negotiations, we were once again served salted and black-peppered boiled chicken and rice. Then, the bride's family made space for the two wedding negotiators, Ntxua, and me to sleep on their living room floor. The rest of the team slept in the van.

Ntxua and I were up at seven to help the bride's family prepare the wedding meal. Soon, the apartment was full of people socializing and drinking. Around eleven, Ntxua, the two negotiators, and I were told to gather in the basement, where a large meal had been prepared. I, again, had a designated spot. I had been told I was supposed to say something to the bride's family at several key points during the wedding, but those instructions had all gone in one ear and out the other. The four wedding negotiators sat at the head of the table, while about thirty others sat in designated seats around the table. One person was there to provide life lessons and wisdom to the groom and bride, and another was there to monitor all the rules and rituals of the wedding, such as ensuring each round of drinks was poured and consumed properly. Everyone present was to avoid putting both hands on the table, crossing their arms or legs, and cursing or saying anything inappropriate. If you violated such a rule, you would either be served an additional two cups of beer or a shot of hard liquor or, if need be, removed from the table and potentially dismissed from the wedding. I ended up sitting near the front of the table, sandwiched between two young men from the bride's side who looked to be about my age.

Soon enough, many rounds of drinking ensued. I just kept drinking and tried not to violate the rules. I tried hard not to put my elbows on the table, cross my arms or legs, drink with the wrong hand, pour with the wrong hand, or say anything that would jeopardize the good fortune of the bride and groom's future.

After several rounds, as everyone ate, drank, and socialized, the groom's wedding negotiators directed the groom and me to get up and walk to one of the corners in the basement. There they told us to stand side by side. Two men from the bride's side then placed a blanket in front of us, to help cushion our knees and hands from the concrete floor. Prior to the ceremony, our wedding negotiators had told us what to do in this situation.

"Bow and kneel to the heavens," one negotiator told us. But before we followed his instructions, we removed the blanket. This gesture signified our commitment to and love for the bride, her family, and their clan, regardless of the difficulties that may lie ahead.

"Bow and kneel to the spirits."

"Bow and kneel to the ancestors."

"Bow and kneel to the grandparents."

"Bow and kneel to the uncles and aunts."

We bowed and kneeled to all the bride's family members who were present at the wedding. At some point, it became so physically demanding, I started asking, "How many more?" After each round of bowing and kneeling, the bride's wedding negotiators told us, "Get up. Get up. That's enough. That's enough. There's no need to do it anymore." But we knew we had to continue. Finally, our negotiator indicated that we could stop, and, exhausted, we returned to our seats.

By the time we got back, many people had left and half of the seats at the table were empty. I thought the hard part was done, but then came the biggest round of drinks yet, intended for me, the groom, the bride's brother, and the bride's cousin. I was shocked when I saw the two bottles of Kessler whiskey set out for this round. *These people must be crazy!* I thought.

After I had poured my two glasses, I said, "Now that your sister is married to us, we are now forever bonded as in-laws. We drink this drink to remember this day for the rest of our lives. We pledge to support and help each other. When you see me in the street, don't forget that I am your brother-in-law. And when I see you on the street, I will not forget that you are my brother-in-law." I then chugged the two glasses of whiskey, filled them up again, and gave them to the bride's cousin. After he chugged them, he filled them up and passed them to the groom. As he did that, he also received two glasses from my brother-in-law, the round from the bride's brother.

When I received two glasses from the bride's brother, I chugged them and instantly vomited. Then my world darkened.

"Take me out," I whispered to ChiaSeng.

Vue then took my place at the table, as ChiaSeng guided me out of the basement. I felt amazing leaving the basement. I felt like a sheet of paper being guided through the air by a cool breeze as I traveled up the stairs, through the living room, through the front yard, and into the parking lot.

"I need to pee." I told ChiaSeng.

"Okay. Do you want to go back in and use the bathroom?"

"No, I need to do it right here, right now."

He stepped aside. As I peed, due to alcohol-induced hallucinations, I looked down and thought I was standing on a huge cliff. Far below, I saw a silent and moving ocean. I had to balance to avoid falling off the cliff.

When I finished, ChiaSeng took me to our van and guided me to the mattress on the floor in the back. They had come prepared.

"Are you okay?" he asked.

"Yes," I told him. "I'm all right."

"Okay then. I'm going back. Hang in there. We shouldn't be too much longer." He then closed the door and left.

Lying alone in the van, away from the ongoing ruckus inside the apartment complex, I had no cares in the world. I could feel the alcohol's electricity running through my veins, from the tips of my toes up to my head. I was floating in outer space. I embraced my oneness with the universe.

When I woke up, we were already back at Ntxua's house on Western Avenue in Green Bay. It was a bit past midnight, the time of night that is the beginning of what the Hmong believe is the transition between the world of the living and the world of the dead. We gathered in the basement where a meal of thinly sliced pork had been prepared. I sat in my assigned seat, next to the bridesmaid. My brother-in-law's family thanked everyone, including me, for a successful wedding. The "thank you" had a rhythm to it, almost ritualistic. Even though it was in Hmong, I didn't understand much of what was being said. Vue and I finally got home around two in the morning.

A few days after this memorable cultural experience, I took some time to reflect. I realized that, as much as I tried to escape it, I would never escape my ancient Hmong world, at least not anytime soon. It didn't matter how Americanized I became, how much my English improved, or how well I did academically. I also realized that even after our refugee community had spent over a decade in the US, our ancient traditions and ways of life were still prevalent throughout Wisconsin and Minnesota, from weddings to funerals, from ceremonies to rituals, and from social and cultural gatherings to politics.

9

One Sunday in August, as I looked through the *Green Bay Press-Gazette* checking the sports section, the cars for sale, the available jobs, and the comics, I came across an ad for the head coach of West De Pere High School's varsity soccer team. Since I was, by that point, familiar with writing resumes and cover letters, I quickly typed up the documents and put them in the mail. I listed my high school coach, Bill Rincon, and my current summer competitive coach, Horst Stemke, as references.

A few days later, I received a call. "Are you still interested in the varsity soccer head coach position?"

"Yes," I told them. "Yes, I am."

I was told to come to the high school for an interview at eleven-thirty the next morning. It wasn't until after I hung up that I realized I would be working at the factory at that time the next day.

The following morning, I put together a set of nice clothes for my interview and placed them in the trunk of the car. Kong and I then went to work as usual. At about ten forty-five, I turned to Kong, who was working next to me, and said, "Hey, I need to leave. When the supervisor asks you where I am, tell her I went outside and that I'll be back after lunch."

"Sounds good, bro," Kong said. "I got your back." He didn't ask anything more.

I went to the restroom, cleaned up, walked to my car in the parking lot, and drove to the high school. The only thing I knew about the West De Pere varsity team was that one of their players had also made the conference team with me the previous year.

I parked, changed clothes in the car, and then walked into the main office.

"How can I help you?" the receptionist asked.

I told her I was there to see the athletic director, Dave Dobkoski.

"Okay. He's expecting you," she said. "Just have a seat there, and he'll come for you."

After a few minutes, a short, stocky man came out of an office and introduced himself as Dave Dobkoski. He led me into his office, where the principal was also seated. The two men asked me questions, and I responded to each, not feeling nervous at all.

Toward the end of the interview, they asked me if I had any questions for them.

"No," I replied, "I don't have any questions." I did wonder if they could smell a pickle odor that followed me from the factory, but I didn't say that out loud.

"We called one of your coaches, and he was very impressed with you," they added.

I thanked them, shook their hands, and dashed out of the office. I changed clothes as quickly as possible in my car and returned to work.

Soon enough, my supervisor approached me and asked why I hadn't been at my station for about two hours. I told her I'd been outside on a long break taking care of some personal issues. I was glad when she told me never to do that again without letting her know. I couldn't have agreed more.

The next day, West De Pere High School called and offered me the job. And, as I had when asked to play varsity soccer and serve as a best man, I said yes without fully knowing what I was getting myself into.

I resigned my position at the pickle factory a few days before the start of my new job at West De Pere. On one of the days in between, Vue asked me to deliver some materials to one of his former colleagues. I met her in a conference room in a downtown hotel. As we talked, she explained that she used to be an elementary teacher, and Vue had been one of the paraprofessionals working in her classroom. She had since resigned from teaching and was training with the motivational speaker Tony Robbins. When I told her I'd never heard of Tony Robbins, she handed me a book and encouraged me to read it in my spare time.

I thanked her and left thinking, *That's interesting, leaving teaching for something else.* Prior to that moment, I had never heard of anyone leaving a profession like teaching for something else. With courage, a person could make a change, even if they were already in a good situation. Later, I read Robbins's book and came away with some ideas that were practical and suited me well. But my meeting with Vue's colleague had a lasting impression on me: even a good life can sometimes be made better.

When I arrived at VFW Park for my new team's first practice, I got a sense of what I would be working with. The field, which was across the street from the high school, wasn't in good condition, and the metal goals were from the 1960s. Our first scheduled game was just two weeks away. I had borrowed Yanghoua's Grand Cherokee, which had enough space for the balls, cones, and other supplies I needed to transport from the school to the field. I wasn't worried about the team's history or past performances. My primary objectives were to evaluate the players, understand their physical and mental capabilities, and then tailor my coaching to their strengths. When it was time, I gathered the players.

"Welcome to West De Pere High School soccer," I started. "I am Coach Lor. It's a pleasure and honor for me to be your coach. I look forward to a great season. The game of soccer is very simple. First and foremost, I don't care about the final score. What I care about is that we prepare well as a team, that we play soccer the right way, and that you don't ever stop competing once the whistle blows. And I'm going to show you how to do that. Got it?"

"Yes, Coach," my players responded.

And with that, practice began. I felt confident as I gave instructions. "Jog as a team, five laps around the field." "Take a water break." "Everyone take a ball and jog five laps around the field. Touch the ball every one to three steps." I led them through stretches and agility drills.

"Running, passing, and positioning make up about 99 percent of the game," I told them. "So, these are the areas we will be working on. Now partner with someone, stand five yards apart, and start passing with only the inside of the foot." I observed. "Now, ten yards apart." I observed. "Now, fifteen yards apart."

We did this for the first week. In the second week, I added movement to passing, and we worked on shooting and scrimmaging. I then showed the team the fundamentals of defense—contain, fight for position to possess the ball, keep everything in front of you, force all plays to the outside, congest the center lane of the field, and do not let your opponent outrun you. I watched each player for their talents, tendencies, and skills so that I could maximize success for the team and for each player.

My coaching philosophy and approach came from my own experiences as a player. I had also coached the local Hmong team for the previous two years, and during that time, I made certain that we had the best players on the field and that each player was the best at their position. Unlike other coaches, I didn't care much for the politics and nepotism of soccer. I particularly enjoyed passing out uniforms because I always loved getting my uniforms as a player. The West De Pere shorts, jerseys, and socks came in white, black, and orange.

Our first two games were against Oshkosh North and Oshkosh West. We got crushed. Between the two games, we scored just one goal. But that goal was one of the happiest moments of my life. I wasn't discouraged. "As long as we leave everything on the field, we are winners," I told the team. "And we did. You gave everything you've got. You were disciplined. And you represented

In the fall of 1990, I became the varsity soccer coach at West De Pere High School. Little did I know that it would be the beginning of a fulfilling career in education and athletics. I am standing fourth from left in the back row.

West De Pere, your parents, and your fans well. That's all that matters. Great job!" As I drove home from the second game, I was already thinking about how to prepare for our first conference game in a week. I knew we didn't have the most talented players in the conference, but we had some good players and some outstanding young people. I had a feeling we would be competitive in every game.

Overall, the season went well. We played up to our potential, losing games to more talented teams and winning games against teams equally or less talented. The team improved with every practice and every game. At the end-of-year banquet, I enjoyed giving out awards to the players and talking about our team, our supporters, and our achievements.

As I reflected on my first season as a coach, I realized I had learned a lot about building a team for success, working with parents, and my coaching philosophy. I also learned that many aspects of coaching came naturally to me. Strategizing, placing players in the right positions, and making key substitutions at key moments—these things felt instinctive to me. Most importantly, I knew my players believed in me.

"Far, we've been traveling far, without a home, but not without a star." The Neil Diamond song "America" played as I clicked through my slides about the Hmong experience—children playing around tribal huts in an isolated mountain village, adults farming rice on steep slopes, distraught families arriving on the Thailand shore of the Mekong River, neighbors gathered at a market in a refugee camp, individuals adapting to American life, and many other pictures of the Hmong diaspora. The room was dark enough that my classmates couldn't tell I was crying. For my final course project in my Family, Kin, and Community class, I'd been able to choose a topic that was relevant to me. The professor was kind and encouraging, and I'd done well in the class. What's more, the research I'd done on the Hmong experience would infuse my life, education, coaching, and teaching moving forward. I was starting to see how my identity, history, education, and work experiences could form the foundation for my future.

I also did well in my Chinese literature course. I could relate to the professor, who was visiting from China, because her native language wasn't English. I had the thought that maybe, one day, I could be like her. I could also relate to the Asian lived experiences and themes covered in the course. Finally, I understood many of the literary techniques utilized by the Chinese authors—they were similar, in some ways, to the Hmong oral storytelling traditions I grew up with. A few other minority faculty and staff members were helping me along my academic journey, including Professor Ron Baba; our Hmong Student Association adviser, Debra Moutry; and my advisor, Cindy Jennings.

Yet, even with their help over three semesters, I hadn't fully acclimated to college. Many of my professors seemed untouchable and distant. I still struggled to understand the importance of majors, minors, and other academic requirements. I felt as though I couldn't quite comprehend certain lectures, assignments, and academic language. At the end of the fall semester, my GPA dipped below a 3.0 for the first time. I continued to walk by Student Services, see familiar names on the dean's list, and think, *Either they know something that I don't, or I simply don't have what it takes to succeed in college.*

10

Near the end of the 1991 spring semester, I came home from class to one of most shocking and devastating discoveries of my life. An anonymous note rested on my bed: "You and Kong need to move out by the end of May." My mind reeled. Kong and I were living in the house with Vue, my sister-in-law, and their two children. Perhaps we had become a nuisance? Perhaps we had not realized that Vue had his own family and could not house us forever? The note was not signed, but I was not concerned with who had written it. I was concerned only with what it meant. *Am I being kicked out of the only family I've known? The only place where I've been welcomed and loved?* I was so overwhelmed, I fell immediately to sleep. When I woke, though I had drained my tears, my spirit was utterly crushed.

I composed myself and crossed the street to my sister's place. When I shared the news with her, she reassured me everything was going to be okay. But I returned home knowing that her support and reassurance wouldn't save me from the dark abyss into which I was falling.

I called Maya and got to her place around midnight. With the money I saved from coaching and work, I had purchased my first car a few months earlier—a 1980 dark blue Datsun, manual 200SX, for $1,400. I picked her up, and we drove all night until we ran out of familiar roads. Then we slept in my car from the morning until early afternoon. I felt so helpless, knowing even my guardian angel couldn't rescue me.

When I got home, I packed up all of my belongings, put them in the car, and drove off. But I had no other place to go. Eventually,

I returned to the house on Third Street and created a small living space for myself in the three-season porch. On the days when I was home, I waited until everyone else had left before I emerged to clean up and then head to class. I tried to stay away from home as much as I could, but it was difficult to let go of my only sense of belonging in this world.

After a few weeks, I moved from the porch to the small office space that was separated from the living room by a set of French doors. While living in this area, I began to hallucinate. On several occasions, I was visited by a dark figure in a black fedora. A few times, he attempted to suffocate me in my bed, smiling as though he was enjoying my demise. Some Hmong people believe visitors like this are dark spirits. I once told Vue about it, and he joked, "That means you're going to get married soon." After I put a knife and a Bible under my pillow, the dark figure did not return.

In the ensuing months, I attended my classes, played soccer on my Hmong team and my competitive travel team, hung out with friends, and attended other social and cultural events, while avoiding home. My coach, teammates, and friends likely didn't notice that my behavior had changed. But deep down, my soul was in a dark well. Except for Yanghoua and Maya, I hadn't told anyone about the anonymous letter. It was too shameful. Too disgraceful. And I didn't dare to tell Kong, knowing how vulnerable he was without another support network. Even unconditional support and love from my sister and girlfriend weren't enough to draw me out of my darkness. I frequently contemplated dropping out of college, shutting my eyes, and staying in the well.

Time passed. The semester ended. One day, though I was still in my darkened well, I walked into the financial aid office and inquired about a summer work-study award. After applying for and receiving the award, I was told I could secure an existing summer work-study position or find my own. However, if I were to find my own job, my employer would need to contribute a

Playing soccer on Team Green Bay, a Hmong team, pictured here at a tournament at UW–Green Bay, was one positive aspect of my life during a difficult time in the early 1990s. I am standing third from left in the back row wearing number 14.

portion of my pay. I reached out to a brother-in-law who was working for Legal Services of Northeastern Wisconsin, a non-profit law firm representing clients at or below the poverty level. The timing turned out to be impeccable. The firm had recently secured a grant for work they planned to do with community elders, and they could use a part of the grant to pay my salary.

In this job, I translated presentations and gave workshops on the legal rights of the elderly. We informed people about housing and tenant policies, age discrimination, and medical services. I learned some important lessons about being a professional, but more importantly, I improved my Hmong because I worked with many Hmong elders. Occasionally, when the court needed an interpreter, I filled this role as well.

One humid summer day, I arrived in court to interpret for a Hmong client who was up for disability benefits. Many Hmong individuals of a certain generation applied for Social Security disability benefits due to the war trauma they experienced in Laos and as refugees in the United States. I was never given any information about my clients until the court hearing. On this day, when my client walked into the courtroom, I realized with a shock that it was my brother Vang. It took me a moment to recognize him because, even on this hot day, he was wearing a winter hat, coat, and boots. His public defender had advised him to wear the gear as a way to support his disabilities case. If I were to reveal my identity, the case would need to be rescheduled, so I carried on as his interpreter without saying anything. Vang also showed no reaction. A few months later, Vang got his disability benefits, which he very much deserved. We never spoke of that day in court. And although Vang was my eldest brother and a father figure to me, I also chose not to share the anonymous letter with him. My siblings and I confided in each other selectively.

Soccer and the job at the law firm kept me busy, which tamed my demons and helped me avoid further psychological deterioration. But I still felt trapped in a vicious cycle of burying and digging myself out of my own grave. I was searching for a spark when eventually a thought came to me: *I will ask Maya if she will marry me.* My intuition told me this would be the right path forward, since I felt an unconditional sense of wellness and happiness when I was with her. But I also had my doubts. *Are my feelings for Maya real or a fluke?* I asked myself. *Is what I have with her truly mutual?* If it wasn't, I didn't want to drag her into my darkness.

Coincidentally, as I began pondering this big decision, two former girlfriends waltzed back into my life. One was Sheng, a girl I had dated a few years earlier. Even though three or four years had passed since we'd last seen each other, it almost felt as though she had never left. I didn't ask her about the man she had left me for, and I didn't expect her to tell me anything. She was still just as beautiful, pleasant, and kind as I remembered. I enjoyed being with her, and the feelings seemed mutual. But when I was with her, I didn't feel the same happiness that I felt with Maya. After a few weeks I finally called her and shared that it wasn't going to work out. A few weeks later, I learned she had gotten married. Many Hmong marriages happened suddenly this way, and I wasn't surprised.

Something very similar happened at about the same time with Blia, who had been my girlfriend when I was eighteen. I ran into her at a social event that I was attending with Maya. When Blia and I had a moment alone together, she pointed to Maya and said, "So, she's the reason why you haven't been responding to my letters or visiting me."

"Yes," I admitted. "I am so sorry." A few weeks later, I learned she had gotten married to an older man from the Twin Cities. Her husband was someone I had run into a few times at various soccer tournaments. Again, the sudden marriage did not surprise me. I was glad my exes and I had reconnected. They gave me an opportunity to envision what my life with and without them would be like. I knew I would be better off with someone else, and I wished them the best on their new journeys.

Having mentally played out the various scenarios of my life hundreds if not thousands of times, I came to a decision about what to do next. On a Saturday morning, I went to visit Maya. When I first arrived, I noticed many cars parked around her family's house, and I panicked. I thought, *No, can she be getting married suddenly just like Sheng and Blia?* Fortunately, the people turned out to be her family members. It was a very nice day, and many of Maya's visiting relatives were hanging out in the backyard.

I met a few people, but I needed to talk to Maya alone. And I didn't have much time because I needed to return home for work. When I found her in the crowd, I immediately asked, "Can we go to the basement? I have something I want to ask you. It won't take long."

"Sure. Let's go," she replied.

In the basement, we sat on her family's flowery cream-colored sofa, and I got right to the point: "What do think about us getting married?"

"Like *married* married?" Maya asked.

"Yes, like *married* married," I answered.

"Are you sure?" she asked, with a smile on her face. "I mean, I think I'm pretty sure, but are you sure?"

"Yes, I'm *sure* sure," I told her.

"Well, if we do it now, it would be a great time," she said. "My brother and his family from Connecticut just arrived, and they will be here for the next two weeks. My stepmom just arrived from Laos and won't be leaving for California for a few weeks. And my aunt from France is also here; so, it would be nice for them to be a part of our wedding."

"Okay. Let's see. How about I pick you up on Thursday evening, August 1, and then we come back for the wedding the following weekend?" We planned to elope, which in Hmong culture entails a groom secretly taking a bride to his house for a spiritual ceremony before the bride's family is notified or a wedding date is agreed upon. It was a common practice for Hmong marriages, and I wanted to honor that tradition.

"Why August 1?"

"Because August 1, 1991, is an easy day to remember. Are you good then?"

"Yes, I think so." Beneath Maya's playful demeanor, I could tell she was processing the seriousness of our decision. She was being practical, but she also seemed exhilarated.

"Okay, then," I said. "I will see you then."

"Yes, see you then."

We went upstairs, and I left.

When I got home, I went to work and then played soccer at Kennedy Park. Later, I was lying on my bed on the porch reading the newspaper when I noticed that Vue was watching television on the sofa in the living room. I decided to sit with him. After a while, I finally asked, "Vue, if I were to get married, what would you think?"

"Well," he said without hesitation, "if you think it's going to be a good thing for you and for your life, getting married shouldn't be an issue."

"Okay, thanks."

"Yeah. Don't worry too much." As usual, our conversation was brief. But Vue's response showed his confidence in my life decisions. He knew me well.

Finally, August 1, the big day, arrived. I worked, played soccer, and talked to a few friends and relatives before heading home. I looked calm, but deep down, I was nervous and full of excitement. I couldn't tell anyone about my feelings, though. We were eloping, and no one knew our plan but me and Maya.

I went home, showered, changed, and headed to Kimberly, arriving at Maya's family home just as the human world was transitioning to the spiritual world. I knew it would be difficult for Maya to sneak out, since she had so many relatives visiting and she was always involved in her family's activities. So, I was excited to see her emerge from the garage alone. She got in my car, and off we went.

"How did you get out?" I asked.

"I told them I forgot to purchase some items for breakfast tomorrow and that I needed to go to the grocery store."

"Okay, that's brilliant."

"Yeah," she smiled. "Wasn't it?"

I didn't know exactly how Maya was feeling, but I was just so happy. "We'll need to stop somewhere to call your family to let them know we're eloping. We don't want them to worry about you or call the cops."

"You're right. Okay."

We stopped at a Burger King and used a payphone to call her

family. Traditionally, a bride's family might not receive news of the elopement for days, depending on the distance between the bride's and groom's families. But this was 1991, we had access to phones, and I wanted to be polite.

"Can I talk to my mom?" Maya asked, and then she paused. "Mom, I wanted you to know that I have left with Pao and that Pao and I are getting married. We are heading to his place. So, please don't worry about me." I couldn't hear her mom's response, but Maya listened patiently to whatever was being said. "Here," Maya said, handing me the receiver. "My mom wants to talk to you."

I got an earful from her mom. She asked if I truly loved her daughter, how I would care for and support her, and if my family and clan would embrace her. I assured her that Maya was in good hands. Then Maya's sister-in-law got on the phone.

"Are you really taking our Maya away from us?" she asked.

"Yes," I replied. "Maya and I are getting married. Please don't worry. She's with me, and she's safe and sound."

But the sister-in-law continued, "Did you know you are taking away our babysitter and cook? Who's now going to watch over our kids and cook their meals?"

Maybe I was not thinking too clearly due to my adrenaline or maybe I was ticked off by her questions, but I replied, "I think that's your business and not ours." A long pause followed. My bluntness had ended our conversation. It was quite a revelation. I had never been so blunt before. I then handed the phone back to Maya, she said her goodbyes, and we headed home.

Driving home this time was different than the other times I'd picked her up and brought her back to Green Bay with me. This time, we understood that our lives were in the process of changing and would never be the same.

As we drove, I worried about the possibility that Maya's family members would come after her before the wedding. I had heard stories of this happening to eloping couples—a bride's family could come after her immediately or even weeks after the news of the elopement.

At the Ashland exit, we stopped at a gas station, and I called my family to deliver the news. I called Vang first, even though I was living with Vue. Maya and I wanted to do a traditional "welcoming the bride" wedding ritual, and it wasn't appropriate to have it at Vue's place because he had converted to Christianity.

"I wanted to let you know that I'm bringing a wife home," I told Vang.

"Okay," he responded calmly. "How long before you get home?"

"Fifteen to twenty minutes," I guessed.

"Okay," he said. "I will call Uncle Nhiachue." When it comes to major life events, like marriage, that have been going on for centuries, certain steps of the process are ingrained and automatic.

I had never visited Vang's house on Shawano Avenue, near Green Bay West High School. He had moved there recently, and I didn't interact much with him or his family at that time. Nonetheless, I was confident he was going to support me. Uncle Nhiachue was already waiting for us at the front door. With cars whizzing by in the background, Maya and I stood at the door while Uncle Nhiachue performed the traditional "welcoming the bride" ritual, which would bless our upcoming wedding ceremony. Since we had no real chickens, Uncle Nhiachue used a bundle of bushes to bless and welcome our spirits:

> Oh, today is a good day, and today is a day of purity. Oh, here, I am blessing Pao and Nyab Pao [my daughter-in-law]. Today, they have chosen to be husband and wife. Let them come to our family, clan, and house without any bad spirits, ills, or intentions. Oh, here, I am warding off all evil spirits that could have followed them or accompanied them home. Oh, ancestors and spirits of the world, here are Pao and Nyab Pao.

> Please protect them. Please give them protection, prosperity, wealth, children, and health, for many years to come in their lasting marriage. Okay, okay, come in, come in.

As we gathered in the living room, my family started asking Maya about her background—her family, her clan, and where they lived in Laos. Uncle Nhiachue then called my cousin Yang and shared with him what was happening. He was to take another person with him and go to Kimberly to let Maya's family know that she was safe and sound with us. That night, Maya and I slept at Vang's house in a small bedroom on the second floor.

We woke up early and went to Vue's house. Maya then helped my sister-in-law prepare boiled chicken and rice for breakfast. After we were all seated at the table, with a lot of commotion, Maya started digging in while the rest of us hadn't picked up our utensils. She noticed, stopped, and looked embarrassed. Her family was Catholic, but not very religious, and they didn't pray during meals. Vue prayed and then we ate.

Later, I took Maya shopping at East Towne Mall. She hadn't brought any clothes to Green Bay. It was also a cultural tradition—a gesture that she had married into a good family that was welcoming and loving and able to provide her with food, shelter, and clothing.

That evening, many of my family members, in-laws, and relatives gathered with us at Vang's place to make plans for the wedding. I shared that the wedding needed to be that coming weekend in order to include Maya's visiting family members. My uncle and some other family members had already assembled my wedding team—one of the benefits of having positive relationships with other clans in the community. My uncle Tongpao Lor and my nephew Nor Xwm Lee were my wedding negotiators, Ntxua was my best man (which was appropriate as I had been his best man), and my cousin, the daughter of my uncle Nhiachue, was the bridesmaid from my side of the family. I was so impressed with how efficiently my uncle had put the wedding team together.

By Friday, August 9, we had gathered enough money for the wedding. My sister and brother-in-law donated three hundred dollars and loaned us seven hundred. One of my cousins and her husband also contributed a thousand, donating two hundred and loaning us eight hundred. My older brothers donated two hundred dollars each. I added seven hundred dollars, which I got from the sale of my Datsun. Other family members and friends donated the rest. Altogether, we had five thousand dollars.

That morning, many of my relatives and friends, along with my wedding team, met at Vang's house. We followed the same process that we had for my brother-in-law's wedding. My best man and I were instructed to bow and kneel many times—to the spirits of the world, the spirits of the house, the ancestors, my grandparents, my parents, my uncles and aunts, and the list went on. Finally, the wedding team got into Yang's blue conversion van, and we headed toward Kimberly. Only Maya and her bridesmaid wore Hmong clothes. We stopped at Sunset Park, less than a mile from Maya's family home, to have our traditional meal of boiled chicken and rice. By tradition, Maya and the bridesmaid each got an entire thigh. When we arrived, the wedding negotiators for both sides exchanged some ceremonial songs before we were allowed entrance. I couldn't grasp the meaning of the songs because the words were so poetic and unfamiliar to me. If there was anything I learned from standing for about two hours, it was patience.

The wedding negotiators discussed various topics until one or so in the morning. One issue was why I took Maya to Vang's house for the welcoming ceremony when I was living with Vue. Her negotiators asked if I had done this because Vue didn't want anything to do with Maya. This wasn't the case—I had taken her to Vang's because Vue was Christian—but I wasn't sure if Maya's family believed us, even after an explanation was given and some money was exchanged. By the end of the long night, our meal of boiled chicken with salt and black pepper and a large bowl of rice mixed with cold water was worth the drama, suspense, and endurance.

The next day, by tradition, my best man and I got up early and helped the in-laws with the wedding feast. By ten o'clock, many people had arrived—mostly family members, but I also recognized a few of my soccer teammates. Around noon, the wedding ceremony began. The protocols were the same as when

Maya and I, along with our wedding party, enjoyed a traditional meal on the way home from our wedding on August 9, 1991. Front row, left to right: Maya's bridesmaid, Ntxawm; Maya; me; and my brother, Vue. Back row, left to right: my wedding negotiator, Norxwm; my cousin and driver, Yang; my best man, Ntxua; my brother, Kong; my brother-in-law, ChiaSeng; and my uncle and wedding negotiator, Tongpao.

I was a best man. There were many rules and many rounds of drinking, followed by more bowing and kneeling. Finally, the clans exchanged thank-yous, Maya and I received a lecture, and then we made our departure. By the time of the lecture, I was too drunk and needed Vue to take my place halfway through. Some family members helped me to the van, where I could rest until the ceremony had ended. Once, a couple came by the van to check me out, since they hadn't met the groom. "Nice looking young man," the woman commented.

We stopped by a wayside before the Scheuring Road exit to again have our traditional meal of boiled, salted, and black-peppered chicken and rice. We were happy and exhausted. It had taken so much to make our wedding successful—from the financial costs and rigid traditions to the physical feats of drinking and kneeling and bowing to the ground. Amidst it all, I maintained a conviction that this was the right path for me. For the first time, I felt genuinely excited about the next chapter of my life.

A few weeks later, we decided to start a family.

11

Maya and I lived with Vue and his family for a month after our wedding, but within the first week, we knew we wanted to move out. Soon enough, we found a place to rent in Oshkosh with a move-in date of September 1, right before the start of the school year. It was a two-bedroom apartment on Titan Court. Maya would attend classes at UW–Oshkosh while I commuted to Green Bay to coach and complete my last semester at UW–Green Bay. Kong would move with us and start his first year of high school at Oshkosh North.

Moving was relatively easy. We could fit all our stuff into Vue's Escort, so we only made one trip. We slept on the carpet until we were able to purchase a bed set from a local thrift shop. Our wedding gifts covered most of our needs—bed sheets, comforters, pots, pans, dishes, flatware, a rice cooker, and various cooking utensils. Maya's mom was kind enough to gift us a new glass dining set, as well as a matching sofa and loveseat. I felt a great relief moving out of the house on Third Street because, of course, I hadn't forgotten about the anonymous letter. Ever since that incident, I felt as if I didn't belong in that house. Whether my sense of being unwanted in that space was perceived or real, it was incredibly powerful. I hoped to never fall into that dark well again.

A few weeks before our move, I'd started my second season coaching varsity soccer at West De Pere High. With many players returning, the team quickly settled into our practice routine and playing style, and the players seemed grounded in the principles I'd taught last year. I was able to increase the intensity of practice and add new drills to refine and advance their skill and execution.

As newlyweds in the fall of 1992, Maya and I captured this photo from the shoreline of Lake Winnebago in Oshkosh.

I enjoyed my first season of coaching so much that I made the decision to major in secondary education. As a reserved and introverted young man, I hadn't previously considered going into teaching. But I knew I wanted to continue to coach high school soccer. The previous spring, I had applied to UW–Green Bay's education program and was rejected for poor grades. Shortly after my wedding, however, I applied to transfer to UW–Oshkosh and was admitted. Even better, I was accepted into their education program. Their willingness to take a risk on me was a great boost to my confidence. They must have seen something in me that UW–Green Bay didn't. I prepared to spend the fall coaching and completing my last semester at Green Bay, knowing that I'd start at Oshkosh that spring.

Our soccer season went extremely well. We didn't get crushed by either Oshkosh North or Oshkosh West, and we won many more conference games than we had the previous year. We beat the usual suspects like Shawano and Marinette and lost to teams like De Pere and other larger Green Bay schools. We concluded the season scoring the most goals in our conference, but we also gave up the most goals. I occasionally felt strange coaching against a few of my former coaches, and it was disorienting to be on the sidelines while some of my former high school teammates were out on the field. But I loved the experience overall. And some of my favorite things about coaching happened off the field, like after away games when restaurants would give me a free meal for bringing the team.

After soccer season ended, Maya and I used my coaching money, along with what we had saved from Maya's work as a nursing assistant, to return the money I had borrowed from my sister and cousin for our wedding. We didn't want to carry too much financial baggage as we started our new life, and we also wanted to prove to my sister and cousin that we were a responsible and conscientious couple.

Soon, we also purchased our first shared vehicle—a 1982, baby blue, two-tone Nissan Maxima. It was listed for $2,600, but we negotiated and got it for $2,200. The owner lived in a well-established neighborhood, and so I figured they must be wealthy with a lot of money saved up. On the other hand, Maya and I were about to give away our life savings, except for the seed money that we received at our wedding. I was shaking as I handed the owner each hundred-dollar bill. I had never handed away that much money to an individual.

Kong lived in our house, but we were all so busy we rarely saw one another. I spent my days commuting, coaching, and attending classes, while Maya worked and attended classes at UW–Oshkosh. Kong was busy adjusting to being a new freshman at Oshkosh North. Sometimes when Maya took a third shift in Appleton, I would go with her, sleep in the car until her shift was over, and then drive her home. She would sleep for the rest of the day while I worked on my schoolwork, exercised, and cleaned and organized the apartment.

When we joined my siblings and their families for this photo in 1992, Maya and I were married and about to start our own family. Among our many nieces and nephews are (back row, left to right) Vue; Vue's wife, May Lee Lor; my brother-in-law ChiaSeng; my sister Yanghoua; me; Maya; Pheng's wife, Ma Lee Lor; and Pheng. Kong, who was single at the time, is in the front row at far right. Vang and his family were not present.

When December rolled around, I resigned from my coaching position in order to focus on our new life in a new place. I also met my UW–Oshkosh academic adviser and registered for my spring classes. I wasn't sure how I would do at this new school, but this much I knew: With a stable environment, I felt revived and renewed. I felt loved. And most importantly, I was going to be a father. I felt like a completely different Pao than I had been just months earlier.

One early morning in May, Maya's water broke. We were still a few weeks away from the due date. We drove immediately to Mercy Medical Hospital. Shortly after we checked in and got settled, a doctor examined Maya and said she was doing well. "Since it's your first child, it may take a while," he told me. "She still has a ways to go."

I explained that I was supposed to take an exam at nine that morning. "If there's nothing urgent at this point, is it possible for me to leave, take the exam, and come back?" I asked.

"That shouldn't be a problem," he said, "especially if you're just going to be gone for a few hours. She will probably be walking for at least another ten hours, if not more. At this point, there's not much to do other than wait."

I left, took my exam, and returned to the hospital before eleven. Maya was still walking, and there had been little progress. She walked for the rest of the day, and I walked with her for almost every step.

Suddenly, as Maya rested between walks, our child's heart rate abruptly dropped. A nurse came rushing in, then more nurses, and then the doctor. Everyone started preparing as though something urgent was about to happen. Suddenly, the doctor handed me a paper and ordered me to sign it.

"I'd like to call my family," I told him.

"You don't have time," he said. "You need to make the decision now."

I signed, and Maya and our unborn child were carted away.

Amid the chaos, I had no idea how much time had passed when the medical staff finally came to get me. They brought me to a room where I greeted our newborn. He wasn't crying or moving like the newborn babies I had seen on TV or the ones we had talked about in our childbirth class. From his chest up, he looked normal, but his lower body was completely purple. Various tubes were connected to him. The class had not prepared me for this moment.

"Have you chosen a name?" a nurse asked.

"Yes," I said. "Sterling Yimleej." When she asked, I spelled it for her.

"Anything you want to say to him?"

"Yes," I said. Then I turned to my child. "Happy to greet you, son. You've found a mom and dad. You've found a home and a family."

The nurses then put him in an incubator. "We're flying him to Theda Clark in Neenah," one of them told me. "You can see him first thing in the morning tomorrow." Then they carted him off. I quickly scanned the room and saw Maya, who was lying helplessly on an operating table. Then I blacked out.

Later, when I woke up, Maya and I were back in our birthing room. I explained to her that Sterling's umbilical cord had been wrapped around his neck and that a C-section had been performed. I stayed with her through the night. In the morning, I left Maya, went home to clean up, and drove to Neenah to see Sterling.

In the ensuing days, my life was split between staying with Maya at Mercy Medical Center and seeing Sterling at Theda Clark. I reassured my siblings and Maya's family and kept them updated. In between, I completed the last week of a summer interim course I had been taking at UW–Oshkosh.

Sterling was almost five pounds. I thought he was tiny until I saw the other newborns in the NICU. Some were the size of my fist, barely over a pound, with incredibly thin skin. Every infant was in an incubator. Sterling could barely eat, and he didn't move much, but at least he was one of the bigger newborns.

I was relieved when Maya was finally discharged. Now, at least the two of us could face this challenge together. I found Maya's resiliency and courage amazing. When we visited Sterling, we were sometimes joined by Vue, Pheng, their wives, my mother-in-law, or Maya's sisters-in-law, who all brought us great comfort. After several weeks, Sterling was discharged.

By mid-June, with Sterling home and doing well after his rough start, I felt like I now had a purpose and a plan. I had someone who loved me, my academics had finally turned a corner, and I was in a stable environment free from negative influences and distractions. I felt as though almost all of the negative energy that had been consuming me was gone.

I decided I would do all I could do to build a good foundation for my family. I couldn't support Maya and Sterling with the jobs I'd had up to that point, like cleaning, washing dishes, lifting packages, telemarketing, and working in a factory.

I now had a better understanding of college requirements, majors and minors, student services, and degrees. In fact, for the first time in my college career, I made the dean's list, earning almost all As in my spring semester courses—a complete reversal from my experience at UW–Green Bay. I achieved those grades while taking a full credit load, plus an additional three-credit interim course.

Importantly, I also had a better understanding of the career I wanted to pursue. Many times, I had paged through the course catalog, reviewing the majors and minors available at UW–Oshkosh. I had envisioned myself in the various professions and lifestyles that different majors and minors might lead to. I now felt confident about my plan to be a teacher and coach high school varsity soccer.

A few months earlier, with our newborn on the way, Maya and I had secured support from Social Services. We now had medical coverage, a monthly check, and a monthly food allowance, eliminating our need to work to support ourselves through college. Maya and I could leave our jobs to more fully invest in our education and future. She held onto her nursing assistant position for as long as she could, and I held onto my job with Sears until the last minute. By May 1992, we had left our jobs and begun dedicating ourselves to our unborn son and our schooling. Now, my next challenge would be deciding exactly what I wanted to teach.

12

In fall of 1992, as I headed into the first semester of my junior year, with almost every aspect of my life now nourishing me, I finally made up my mind. I was going to study English education and literature—my most challenging and unfamiliar academic subjects by far, but also the ones I found most interesting. I figured, even in the worst-case scenario, I would still be improving my communication skills, my general knowledge of the human condition, and my chances of coaching high school soccer. To balance out this academic challenge, I minored in coaching athletics, my strength.

I had been thinking about this decision since the start of the summer when I began a work-study position at the UW–Oshkosh Post Office. The post office workers, who were mostly in their late forties and early fifties, graciously shared with me their life stories and lessons, where they had grown up and where they had previously worked, along with many other things. Sorting through the mail taught me a lot about the different academic departments, faculty, and staff at the university, as well as where everything was located. When my work-study job ended, I felt deeply enriched by the stories of my post office coworkers. Most of all, I was grateful that I had a wonderful family to go home to.

While I continued to attend Oshkosh as a full-time student, Maya started going part-time that fall. She had switched her major from nursing to social work because after a few weeks of her nursing clinical, she didn't feel nursing would be the right profession for her. In October, we moved from our Titan Court apartment to West Snell Road, on the outskirts of Oshkosh, near Winnebago

County Park. We didn't like the congested feel of the city, so we moved out of town to be closer to nature. Kong had moved back in with Vue before the start of the school year. Another resident in our apartment complex was a Hmong student at UW–Oshkosh, and she had a white roommate. We found this intriguing because it was so uncommon.

About halfway through the semester, I started to find my education and literature courses enlightening and transformative. I loved learning about the US educational system and its roles in changing and advancing both individuals and society. In my literature classes, I appreciated the independent thinking and the process of considering texts through different perspectives and lenses. Unlike some of my prior courses that didn't seem relevant to my life, English made sense to me. I even came to enjoy group work and interactions with my professors and classmates. In fact, a few professors had started to seem less like robots and more like humans in my eyes. A few classmates had even become friends. My education was no longer simply happening to me. I was now becoming a part of it.

Winter came, and the weather grew so cold that our two cars—a Nissan Stanza and a Toyota Celica—both died. A while back, we had sold our Maxima to a Hmong family that needed a vehicle. We added that money to some more we had saved up to buy the 1987 Stanza GXE, which was also baby blue. But apparently it was no match for Oshkosh winters. I took a taxi to campus so I wouldn't miss any classes.

For the first six months of Sterling's life, Maya and I took him to the hospital frequently, sometimes once a week and sometimes multiple times a week. He experienced many health issues—fevers, eczema, ear infections, diarrhea, low appetite, digestion problems, and erratic breathing. It was worrisome, to say the least.

One wintry evening, with the temperature below zero degrees, we took him to the emergency room with a high fever that had been intensifying for several days. The hospital staff told us many kids his age were also having the same high fever and symptoms, and that a few of them were found to have meningitis. To be sure Sterling didn't have it, they would need to do a meningitis test, which would involve injecting a needle into his spine to extract some liquid for testing. When the doctor told us that there was a 1 percent chance that the needle could hit a nerve and paralyze him, we became emotionally overwhelmed and couldn't go through with the procedure.

Late that evening, we drove to Green Bay to see one of my aunts who was a shaman. We planned to stay overnight, and she would perform a shamanistic ritual the next morning to see what could be causing his illness. The temperature continued to plummet until it was down to double digits below zero. Though we slept in my aunt's house under three heavy layers of blankets, it still felt like we were sleeping outside. Even in such extreme temperatures, Sterling was still burning up inside his clothes and snowsuit.

I awoke from sleep when Sterling started crying profusely. I looked at my watch. It was two in the morning. I checked his fever, and it was the same. Ten minutes passed, and he didn't stop crying. It didn't seem like he was going to stop anytime soon.

Disturbed by the commotion, my aunt woke up and told us she would perform the ritual immediately. She set up her altar and began. As my uncle observed the ritual, he occasionally burned a few sheets of spiritual paper money into a metal bowl. Though I didn't understand what was going on, I was just hoping it would work.

My aunt entered a trance, moving her arms and legs in repetitive motions. Then she began chanting, communicating with spirits and ancestral guides to discover the source of Sterling's illness. After over an hour, she was done. She continued to sit peacefully on the long wooden bench where she had been sitting for the last hour and a half. My uncle then got up and massaged her shoulder.

Finally, she gathered herself, removed the hooded red sheet that had been covering her face, and told Maya and I to bring Sterling over. We sat on the wooden bench facing the altar and held Sterling in front of us. Incense sticks, a bowl of rice, a few shots of alcohol, and paper money neatly covered various parts of the altar.

She took a sip from a bowl of water and then blew water all over Sterling's head. Then she took several red strings and tied them around his ankles, wrists, and neck. These were to protect him from evil spirits.

"Everything is going to be fine," she assured us. "Let's go back to bed."

All of us, including Sterling, slept peacefully for the rest of the morning. After breakfast, we thanked my aunt and uncle for their support. As we drove back to Oshkosh, Sterling's fever dissipated. We were thankful we didn't have to do the meningitis procedure.

Shortly after the spring semester started, I applied for another work-study position. This one was with the Anchorage Youth Program at Winnebago Mental Health Institute, which was a secure residential program for adolescents with psychiatric disorders, behavioral disorders, and substance abuse issues. I was intrigued by the position and thought it would be an incredible experience.

Dale Malesevich, the director, interviewed me and hired me for the part-time job on the spot. My regular shift would be from three in the afternoon to eleven at night, and if they needed extra help on the weekends, I would occasionally cover the eleven p.m. to seven a.m. shift.

"I will be there for certain," I told him.

"Pao, there are only two things in life that are certain: death and taxes," he said, laughing. "I will see you then." Dale had a sense of humor, which, as it turned out, was needed to work at Anchorage.

After a few months, I came to respect and appreciate the staff. Dale was a flexible and knowledgeable director. John, one of the counselors, was calm and gentle. Rachel, on the other hand, was a no-nonsense counselor who disciplined with tough love. Other counselors fell somewhere in between John and Rachel on the spectrum. Many patients were court ordered to be there. They came from all over the state and from various upbringings, yet all had scars, torments, and pains that I wasn't sure they could ever be healed from. I could relate to them in some ways, but I knew I would never fully understand their experiences.

Brandon was always angry at something or someone. Marshall was a genius but couldn't stop harming himself because of his inner demons. Sarah didn't last long because she constantly peed and pooped in her room and smeared her excrement all over the wall, floor, and door. Elizabeth was kicked out after a week because her parents had given her marijuana during visiting hours. Samantha was reserved and always in her own world where few, if any, could reach her. And there were others with their own particular struggles and suffering.

Their days and activities were structured down to the minute and second, as were my days. Go to classes. Go to work at Anchorage. Return home. And in between, take Sterling to the hospital and attend to various family obligations.

I couldn't wait until spring and summer when I could play soccer with other players at Menominee Park. In the meantime, I had been going to the Kolf Sports Center at noon to work out and occasionally play pickup basketball. One day, one of the staff members who worked in Dempsey Hall stopped coming to our games. I asked one of the professors, "Where's Randy?"

"He left the university. He retired to work on his hobbies."

"But he's not that old."

"Yep. But his hobbies generate enough income for him to leave his job."

I was surprised to hear that. I had always thought everyone worked until they reached sixty or sixty-five and then retired. As I made my way home, I decided, *I want to be like Randy. Someday, I'd like to leave work on my own terms, not dictated by age.*

13

"Go, go, go!" Someone guided us, as we had rehearsed, up several flights of stairs and then into the fieldhouse. Before the frenzy, as I waited in line with the rest of my classmates and had a few moments to reflect, I had wished so badly that my parents could be there. I hadn't thought about them in a while. But thinking about them on the day I was graduating from college, I had to control my emotions to stop from crying.

Music consumed the fieldhouse, amplified by the large crowd applauding and yelling. It was empowering and inspirational. I couldn't help but soak in the moment—I couldn't believe I had made it. Now, I just had to make certain I wouldn't faint or fall while walking across the stage.

I looked for my family, but there were too many people. So, I followed directions and found my seat. Not long after the ceremony began, I was already thinking about when it would end. Rather than paying attention to the graduation speakers, I was thinking about how to avoid falling flat on my face when my turn came to walk across the stage.

Before I knew it, I was standing near the steps to the stage. I didn't like hearing my name called or walking across the stage, but I was swept up by the moment. After the ceremony, Vue, Pheng, Yanghoua, their families, and I stopped and ate at a local Chinese buffet. Then everyone departed.

I had no celebration party planned, and I'd shared with my siblings that I didn't want one. I very much appreciated that they respected my wishes. I felt an immense sense of pride and relief upon finally earning my bachelor's degree—and I was confident

Before my UW–Oshkosh graduation ceremony in 1994, my family members gathered to celebrate at our home. Back row, left to right: Pheng holding his son Ntswjtug, me holding Sterling, and Vue. Front row, left to right: Ma Lee Lor, Pheng's wife, holding their daughter Sia; Maya; and May Lee Lor, Vue's wife.

that my relatives were equally euphoric. To me, the most important celebration happened earlier that day when my siblings and their families arrived at our apartment, and I got to put on my cap and gown and take pictures with them. Those pictures—of me with my siblings, their spouses, my nieces and nephews, and Maya and Sterling—remain some of my most treasured photographs.

In the summer of 1994, Sterling turned two, and suddenly everything changed. He was no longer sick. No more doctor visits. No more spiritual ceremonies, practices, or rituals. When I was free during the day, Sterling and I would walk to Winnebago County Park and fish. Sometimes he would watch me practice soccer.

When June came, I flew to Washington, DC, to participate in a leadership fellowship program. I hadn't been on a plane since my family's flight to Long Beach from Bangkok, Thailand, in 1980. Two nieces, one from my side of the family and the other from Maya's side, planned to stay with Maya and Sterling until my return.

Back in March, I'd learned about the program, applied, and received an acceptance. It was a two-month leadership experience, all expenses paid. Months ago, I'd also decided to postpone my student teaching in order to attend graduate school. I was going to get my master of science degree in educational leadership at UW–Oshkosh, a thirty-six-credit graduate program. Since I had already taken fifteen graduate credits as part of my undergraduate degree, I only needed twenty-one additional credits to earn my master's. I had also received a Chancellor's Award for Diversity that would support my graduate study. Despite my lingering doubts about my place in the world, I was beginning to notice signs guiding me toward an unexpected career in teaching and leadership.

Before leaving for DC, I asked my graduate program director if I could do an independent study during my fellowship to earn some credits. A faculty member was willing to work with me, and we came up with a three-credit leadership project. By the time I started the program in the fall of 1994, I would need to complete just eighteen credits.

The other fellows and I were housed in a complex in the southeast area of DC, which I had heard was one of the most dangerous areas, not just in DC, but in the country. It had one of the highest per capita murder rates in the world. My roommates Frank, who was Chinese American, and Gary, who was Mexican American, were from California. Other leadership fellows came from Texas, Colorado, Florida, Minnesota, and Wyoming, among other states. The program directors told us to never go anywhere alone and never go out after eight at night. We even had a grocery store and a laundromat in the basement of the complex, meaning we rarely needed to leave our building. I took the metro to my fellowship at the National Council for Educational Opportunity, a lobbyist group working to support TRIO Programs. When I was a student at UW–Oshkosh, I'd benefited from a TRIO program. These federal outreach programs existed to support students from disadvantaged backgrounds.

During our spare time, Frank, Gary, and I visited various monuments and toured some of the DC neighborhoods. One day, we ventured into other parts of the southeast area, which hadn't changed much since the 1950s and 1960s. I got a haircut in a barbershop that had red leather seats from the 1950s. It was the longest haircut I ever had, over an hour, but the barber was meticulous, taking his time with the clippers, powder, and razor. All the while, he was talking with other barbers and clients. On Sunday mornings, while Frank and Gary hung out in our room, I went to the National Mall and played pickup soccer. I was thrilled to be playing with so many players from around the world.

One day, when we all returned home from our fellowship sites, Gary told us he had gotten three tickets to a FIFA World Cup game at RFK Stadium. It was Holland versus Saudi Arabia. Someone at his fellowship site, which was at the White House, wasn't going to attend, so Gary gladly took the tickets. When we arrived, RFK Stadium was teeming with people and the atmosphere was electric. Fans had their faces painted, music filled the air, and vibrant flags waved from every corner of the stadium. Once the game started, I was captivated by the fast pace of play and the enthusiastic reactions of the fans.

On another day, on my way home from my fellowship site, I ran into a Hmong person from South Carolina. I was shocked. I couldn't believe I was meeting another Hmong person in DC. We chatted, and I learned he was working for the Department of Health and Human Services. The Hmong community hadn't been in the US for very long, so it hadn't occurred to me that a Hmong individual could already hold a prestigious position within the federal government. "Until now, I have never ventured out of Wisconsin, other than visiting Minnesota and Illinois," I told him.

He replied, "You know, sometimes we just need to step outside of our comfort zone and experience the world." I felt that I couldn't agree more.

A few times a week, the other fellows and I would attend special events, mostly meeting and listening to prominent leaders from underrepresented groups. I was intrigued by the opening remarks of a Latino judge from one of the local courts: "Some people say, if you are motivated, you can do anything! Well, let me tell you. This is a great lie. Let me share with you the real formula for success. Performance and success in life are equal to expectations times motivation times ability." Wow, that made sense to me! I had never heard of success being framed that way. I decided I would add one more element, though—along with expectations, motivation, and ability, one also needs some luck.

This trip was my first time away from my family, and after five weeks, I got homesick. I had a few days off from my fellowship during the Fourth of July week, so I reached out to Dr. Hawkins, the vice-chancellor for academic support at UW–Oshkosh, to see if the university could purchase a round-trip plane ticket for me to return home. I was incredibly relieved when she said, "Yes, we can do that." I was so glad to see Maya, Sterling, and other family members. We attended the Oshkosh Sawdust Days festival at Menominee Park, where I couldn't wait to have my favorite treat: a large piece of fried bread called a tiger paw. We also went to Ripon to help Yanghoua, who was working as a food vendor at the local fair. Her daughter, who had been staying with Maya and Sterling while I was in DC, also came along.

I returned to DC with mixed feelings. I had learned that

working on federal policies and governance can make one feel very removed from the people those policies impact. While I was interested in the work, I looked forward to returning to Maya, Sterling, and the rest of my support network.

When fall came, I started my graduate program. I also became a graduate assistant with the department, taking minutes at meetings and running the computer lab. I gradually learned how the department functioned and came to see the professors in a new light. In this more informal environment, they were more personable than when I had them in classes.

After a year, Maya, Sterling, and I moved to Appleton to be closer to Maya's mom, who had been helping us out with babysitting. My mother-in-law got married when she was about fifteen years old, which was typical of her generation. Sadly, her husband was assassinated in Laos in 1967. She didn't remarry so she could focus on taking care of her three sons and her two youngest daughters. Later, she took care of her many grandchildren, and now she cares for her great-grandchildren. She has done it all with grace, dignity, and compassion. What an amazing woman.

In the fall of 1995, we were expecting our second child. After my anticipated graduation in December, I planned to student teach in the Appleton area in the spring. We found a small apartment on Kensington Avenue, just a few blocks from my mother-in-law. For the next couple of months, I commuted to UW–Oshkosh to complete my courses and finish my semester as a graduate assistant.

In mid-December, Maya, Sterling, my siblings and their families, and some friends and relatives returned to Kolf Sports Center for another graduation. But this time, I didn't feel the same profound sense of accomplishment that I'd felt getting my bachelor's degree. Everyone once again met up at a Chinese buffet, ate, and departed. Vang and his family couldn't attend. I wished they could have.

In March, we welcomed our second child—Phenix—into our family. After what had happened with Sterling, it took me and Maya a few years to heal and gather the courage to have another child. We had consulted our doctor about the chances of having another C-section, and then we took our fifty-fifty chance. Phenix wasn't breech, and all went well. We were most joyful. Now, I had one last academic stop—student teaching—before heading off to start my new career and life.

"Sorry, Pao, but I just don't think you will do well as a middle or high school teacher. Your English isn't adequate. You will face many challenges, and I don't know if you will be able to handle them." My cooperating teacher spoke these words to me after a classroom observation during my second student teaching placement in June 1996. Though I looked calm on the outside, I was devastated on the inside. I had planned my entire future around a career as a high school teacher and varsity soccer head coach, and I had no alternative plans. Also, because this was happening during my final student-teaching meeting with my cooperating teacher and university supervisor, there was no time to pivot.

Lost and confused, I didn't share the feedback with anyone, not even Maya. I endured the last week of student teaching, which easily felt like the longest week of my life. Based on their feedback, I thought I might not ever teach again. It was disheartening. After almost five months in the trenches of the teaching profession, I had slowly but surely found answers to the many questions I'd had about teaching back in January. Before I started, I wondered: *What will happen if there is a fight in my class? How will I handle angry parents? Will the other teachers be smarter or better teachers than me? How will I know I am an effective teacher?* In short, *Do I really have the knowledge, skills, and disposition to be a middle or high school teacher?* I thought I had determined that the answer was yes. The encouraging interactions I had with my students made me incredibly excited about my career choice. But now, my supervisors were telling me I was wrong.

Fortunately, I had a bit of a backup plan. Back in March, after Phenix was born, Dr. Hawkins had invited me to her office for a meeting. "In the last four years, you've accomplished quite a lot here as a student," she told me. "I wanted to let you know that we have noticed. That's the reason I invited you here. It is to see if you would be interested in an opportunity working for the Division of Academic Support."

"Wow, Dr. Hawkins, thank you so much," I said, in shock. "What is the opportunity?"

"Well, you have two options. One is working for Multicultural Services as an adviser. As a student of color at Oshkosh, you have a lot to share from your experience here over the last four years. Or two, you could work as an academic adviser for Student Support Services, something your experience here will also have prepared you to do."

"If I were to choose one or the other, when would I start?"

"June," she answered. "Once you're done with student teaching."

I considered this for a moment. Then I said, "Teaching is still my goal. What if I started working here and then found a teaching job? Would it be okay for me to then leave, after just a few months? It's just that I've always wanted teaching to be my career."

"That's perfectly understandable," she said. "Yes, of course, if you were to find a teaching position, I would be supportive of your leaving. It's understandable."

I asked if I could have a few days to think about it, and she said yes.

"Thank you for the opportunity and for thinking of me," I said before leaving her office.

"You earned it, Pao," she told me. "You earned it."

The following week, I accepted Dr. Hawkins's offer and

decided to take the academic adviser position working with Saroj Thekkanath, who had been my adviser and was now the director of Student Support Services.

Between April and June, I still completed three teaching applications and sent them to Oshkosh, Appleton, and Green Bay. I focused on these school districts because Maya was still completing her social work program at Oshkosh. Plus, we needed her mom's help babysitting Sterling and Phenix. But no matter what happened with the applications, I had the comfort of knowing a job waited for me after student teaching. I was beginning to see how these moments of doors opening and closing were a glimpse into the dynamics of the working world. And with a job with benefits in my future, Maya and I would no longer need to receive housing assistance, medical support, food stamps, or a monthly check from Social Services. We were incredibly grateful for all of the state and local programs that had supported us for three years.

PART III

The Journey

Darkness within darkness.
The gate to all mystery.
—Lao Tzu

14

My first professional job couldn't have started any more smoothly. As a student, I had received valuable mentorship from Director Thekkanath, as well as others who were now my colleagues in Student Support Services. I felt comforted by their presence and support. Also, with my recent bachelor's and master's degrees, I felt confident that I could help undergraduate students with their academic schedules, personal challenges, financial aid decisions, and career planning.

Yet, I still hoped to find a job as a teacher. So, throughout June and July of 1996, I had a few interviews with surrounding school districts. Two were for English as a Second Language positions, which I wasn't certified to teach, and one was for a reading position. I was offered the reading position, but since it was a one-year conditional contract, I consulted with a mentor and decided not to take it. The teacher was on leave and would return the following year, which meant I would need to look for a new job. As for the other two positions, I learned that the in-house candidates had been hired and that my interviews were just a formality. Those experiences showed me the power of informal professional networks. In some ways, that was how I'd gotten my position with Student Support Services, too.

I didn't apply to any teaching positions for the rest of the summer. I was happy in my job at UW–Oshkosh, and in my spare time, I continued to play soccer at Hoover Park and sometimes at Memorial Park in Appleton, hang out with family and friends, and appreciate my joy-filled life with Maya, Sterling, and Phenix.

In October, Maya and I moved into Maya's brother's house

on Welhouse Drive, where we had our wedding back in 1991. Her brother's family had moved to Big Rapids, Michigan, to run a Chinese restaurant. Maya's mom moved in with us to help us care for five-year-old Sterling and Phenix, who was now one.

Earlier that spring, my UW–Oshkosh professor Dr. Scherie Lampe had encouraged me to apply to UW–Madison's educational administration doctoral program, where she had earned her doctoral degree. Out of respect for her, I applied, but I fully anticipated that I would be rejected. *What UW–Madison doctoral program would accept a twenty-four-year-old Hmong refugee with a green card?* I wondered. But over the summer, I was shocked to learn I had been accepted. At first, I didn't follow through, because I had been offered no financial support. Then, I learned I'd received an Advanced Opportunity Fellowship, which would cover my tuition for the first two years of the program. If I were to make it to my third year and beyond, my program of study would pay for my tuition after that. Because my heart was still set on teaching, I had been applying for teaching positions while working at UW–Oshkosh, and I'd even interviewed for two positions in Madison and scheduled a few more. But when the financial support for my doctoral study was confirmed, I canceled my interviews and withdrew my applications from consideration. I was thrilled about this new opportunity, but like many things thus far in my life, I wasn't so sure what I had gotten myself into.

To secure financial support, I had postponed my enrollment in graduate school until the fall of 1997, so I continued my work at Oshkosh in the fall of 1996. Since my position was classified as limited-term employment, the university had to officially post it again after six months. I went through the interview process again and was officially hired on an annual contract. A part of me felt horrible for the other candidates who had applied and interviewed for the position.

Having recently graduated and experienced some realities of

the professional world, I was in an excellent position to support students as they navigated their academic journeys and explored their career goals while also handling various personal challenges. After just six months, I could sense the elevated confidence, competence, and self-esteem of my advisees. I also learned so much from them. Chad from Canada hoped to work with the Canadian secret service, and he promised he would support me if I ever needed safety in Canada. Chong sold me his AIWA stereo system before returning home and promised to show me the life and culture of his home country, Singapore, if I ever visited. I bonded with Kerry, a football player from Jamaica, over our shared interest in athletics and the cultural challenges we both faced on campus and in the community. I showed my advisees—particularly those in minority groups—that professors can be personable. I helped them establish relationships with professors and staff for future references, and I encouraged them to request exceptions outside of university policies about grades and assignments due to the particular challenges they faced.

In the fall of 1997, I drove to work at Oshkosh during the day, and then two or three times a week, I would drive to Madison for my classes, which started at 7:15 p.m. and ended at 10:15 p.m. During the non-winter months, I typically arrived home around one in the morning. In the winter, with snowstorms and icy conditions slowing my drive, I'd get home closer to two. Then I'd wake up early the next morning and head to work in Oshkosh. By the end of the academic year in the spring of 1998, I was relieved to have blundered my way through my courses, but I was even more relieved to have avoided all the deer, bad drivers, and other dangers threatening to crash into my car or send me flying off the road.

That fall, Maya and I also made a big life decision. We purchased land on Christopher Lane where we planned to build a house. With our jobs secured, and having saved enough money for a downpayment, we felt it was time for us to move into the next phase of our life together—home ownership. We looked forward to having a place for our family to grow. Construction started in December.

The spring of 1998 was busy but exciting. In late January, Maya's sister Mai Jongpao, her husband, and their youngest child emigrated from France and moved in with us. Maya's brother Vang was their sponsor. It had been more than ten years since they put in their immigration application to relocate to the United States. If it hadn't been for Maya, they likely would have waited another ten years—or even longer—for their opportunity to come to the country. Back in January 1997, Maya accepted an offer to be a social worker for Outagamie County, and during one of her interagency meetings, she met a representative from Senator Herb Kohl's office and inquired about her sister's immigration status. The representative followed up on the paperwork and discovered that a notice had been sent to Maya's sister and her family, but because they had moved, they'd never received the notice. Maya's chance meeting with the senator's representative sped up the immigration process. They lived with us for a month and then moved to the Twin Cities to join their clan families.

In March, Maya and I welcomed our third child, Chynna, into our family. There were no complications, and the experience was joyful. Then, in April, construction on our new house on Christopher Lane was completed, and we finally moved in. We were able to find a tenant for Maya's brother's house so that his family didn't have to pay the mortgage.

In the summer of 1998, a chance conversation with a fellow student during one of my classes at UW–Madison ended up having a major influence on my life. When this student, Don Schlomann, overheard me discussing my teaching license in a conversation with another student, he joined in to ask me some follow-up questions.

"Are you looking for a teaching position?" he asked.

"Yes," I told him, "but so far, no takers. Just a few interviews here and there and an offer that wasn't a good fit."

"How about Appleton? Have you applied there?"

"Yes," I said, "I did, but I'm not anticipating a response."

"If I could pull something together, would you be interested in teaching for Appleton?"

I was taken aback by this question, but I answered honestly. "Yes, absolutely, I would consider it. It's where my family and I are living now."

"Okay," he said. "I'll get back to you tomorrow."

Our class resumed, and we listened to more lectures and participated in small group activities. The two-hour ride home was a blur. I couldn't wait until tomorrow's class. At the time, I had no idea how such an informal conversation could lead to an actual job. It wasn't until later that I learned Don's job as an assistant superintendent meant he was responsible for recruiting teaching talent for the Appleton Area School District.

I was on the road by five the next morning to arrive in time for my eight o'clock class. Before class started, Don found me. "Here's the situation, Pao," he explained. "Appleton East has four sections of two preps open. We just need to find one more section in another Appleton school to make you full-time, which we can do. Is this good for you?"

I had no idea what he meant by *sections* and *preps*, but I was ecstatic and replied, "Yes, yes, that would be great!"

"You'll need to call Becky VandeHey at East and arrange for an interview. But don't worry—they'll be expecting you."

As soon as I got home, I called and arranged for a late afternoon meeting the next day. Becky, who was the associate principal for curriculum and instruction, and I discussed the courses I would teach, and she gave me a tour of East High School, which was a lot bigger than I had imagined. During the tour, I met a Hmong man working in the cafeteria who'd often played soccer with me at Memorial Park. After the tour, Becky told me to expect a contract in the mail. After I signed and returned it, she explained, I would receive a letter about orientation and onboarding. With that, I was on the path to realize my dream of becoming a high school teacher. Needless to say, I was filled with excitement and anxiety.

Dr. Hawkins and Saroj Thekkanath were not surprised when I informed them of my forthcoming departure, and they expressed gratitude for the two years I had given them. They must have known me better than I knew myself, because I had fully anticipated staying at the university. In fact, I had already taken courses in higher educational administration and curriculum at UW–Madison, and I'd just signed up for more. But I simply could not say no to this opportunity. It was my dream—a dream that I had been told was impossible two years earlier. Yet, I had thoroughly enjoyed my time as a university adviser, and as I turned in my resignation letter, I hoped that one day I would return to the university and possibly even end my career there. Anything after that would be on my own terms, just like my teammate Randy from pickup basketball years ago who had retired early.

About a week before my first day as a teacher, I played pickup soccer at Hoover Park, as usual. But on that day, I felt different. Though my body was executing plays, my mind was elsewhere. It was almost as if I could watch myself playing soccer. Kids ran around, their parents relaxed, people played baseball and volleyball in the distance, cars pulled into driveways, and dogs strained on their leashes. All the while, my heart raced as blood pumped through my veins. My dream was about to become a reality.

15

Before the students of Appleton East and Appleton North came back to school for their fall 1998 semester, I started my first week as a teacher. Barry Bauschek, a retired teacher, helped me with onboarding, showing me how to use my computer, check email, take attendance electronically, operate the overhead projector, and utilize library resources, among many other things. He was one of the kindest and most inspirational people I'd ever met, reminding me of Yoda from *Star Wars*. I surveyed my classrooms, envisioning how they would look full of students. I then attended my first teacher in-service day, though much of what I learned there I quickly forgot.

For weeks now, after signing my contract and learning the courses I would teach, I had been planning, designing, refining, and finalizing units for each course. I needed to prepare materials for three different courses, and I wanted to make my plans flexible enough that I could adjust things based on my students' needs. I'd be teaching one first-year communication arts class to highly motivated students and another to high-need students, who might be unhoused, court-ordered, bilingual, and/or bicultural. My two American literature and composition courses were intended for juniors. My technical writing and computer application course was for seniors planning to go directly into a career after high school.

I worked hard to incorporate a variety of learning activities into my units, including visits to the computer lab and the library and even field trips to relevant community or state events. I wanted everything to be engaging and relevant for each student.

And I wanted to include learning opportunities that I, too, would enjoy. My goal was to be myself—an authentic and personable professional. I was driven to treat each student with dignity and respect, with no exceptions.

Here we go! I thought to myself as I awoke with excitement and uncertainty swirling inside me. This was the first day of a new professional journey, and I could feel the weight of its significance. I went through my morning routine—brushing my teeth, taking a shower, and choosing simple attire to avoid standing out.

Arriving early at East High School, I paused to calm my nerves and absorb the atmosphere. The school felt both familiar and foreign, a place where countless stories had unfolded and where mine was just beginning. I meticulously prepared my classroom. As I watched the students arrive, my heart swelled with a mix of hope and responsibility. I had the potential to make a difference in each of their lives. As they entered the classroom and took their seats, I felt a profound sense of readiness. This was more than just a job; it was a journey we were starting together, and I was eager to see where it would lead us.

After a few weeks of teaching, I realized I had been conditioned by the school bell, which rang at the start of each school day, the start and end of each class, and the end of the day. The first bell snapped me into my teaching zone, and the last bell snapped me back into my role as a father, husband, and community member. During each class, I knew there could be moments of brilliance or moments of chaos that could impact a student for a lifetime. The students and I were responsible for creating brilliant moments and minimizing the chaos. But in order to achieve this, I needed to establish an environment where such teamwork could thrive.

Things were going pretty well until three months into the semester when I received my first phone call from a parent. As usual, I was in my office during my nonteaching hour before lunch. The time was sacred to me, but I had informed students and parents that they could reach me during this hour, so I was always ready to address concerns or questions.

"I'm Mr. Vandenbush," the parent said. "I'm calling because my kid, Sam, isn't doing well in your class, and he said it's all your fault."

"Thank you for calling," I responded. "Can you share more details?"

"Sam said he doesn't understand you and that you kick him out of the class because you don't like him."

I knew the student well and had a good idea of what he may have relayed to his father. "Yes," I agreed. "He is not doing well. Many of his scores are low, barely passing. And yes, I removed him from the class because he was disrupting the learning of other students."

Mr. Vandenbush continued, "He also said that you accused him of cheating, and that's why he got a zero on some of the tests."

"That is true," I replied. "He did cheat on a few of his tests, and getting a zero for cheating is the class policy."

"Well, you better do something about it!" I felt him becoming angrier, but I remained patient.

"Mr. Vandenbush, I will continue to work with him."

"I think you're treating him badly because you don't like him."

"Mr. Vandenbush, if you're not willing to discuss how you and I can support your son, and given your tone of voice, I'm going to hang up."

"What?" he asked in disbelief. "So, now you're going to hang up on me?"

"Yes," I said firmly. "I'm going to hang up on you, and you can call me back when you are ready to discuss how you and I can support your son."

I set down the receiver and ended our conversation. A few minutes later, he called back, apologized, and shared the challenges that he and his wife were having with their son. I listened. Then I asked him to encourage his son to behave in the class. He needed to improve his behavior in order to improve his grades and for us to continue to support him. Within a few weeks, the student's behavior and grades improved, and I never got another call from his father.

In March 1999, I found myself at the Appleton Area School District job bidding fair, an event set up to give current employees like me first dibs at positions throughout the district that would become available the following school year. I attended because I was interested in finding a position that would put me at one school instead of two. When positions were announced, any interested teachers lined up in an order based on their licensing certifications and seniority. When they announced the position I desired, teaching eighth grade communication arts, I lined up to see if I could secure it. To my great surprise, I did. By taking this new position, I gave up my current position for the following school year.

Pleased with this result, I walked back to my seat to gather my things. But all of a sudden, an administrator from another school approached me, demanding, "Are you sure you want to take this position?" I had been warned about this administrator, so his unprofessional demeanor didn't surprise me. Apparently, he was the type to abuse his position of power.

"Yes, I am taking this position." I replied. *How dare you even ask me this question?* I thought. After all, my life and career were at stake, and I had a family to support, though that was surely the least of his concerns.

"Well, you better not be playing games," he added. His rude tone may not have surprised me, but this blatant threat did. I hadn't come to the fair expecting to be bullied—especially among individuals who work with students, families, and educators. He was surrounded by a team of teachers from his school, reminding me of the bullies and gangs I'd dealt with on the school playground and in my community growing up. I suspected they already had someone in mind for the position. I understood that they wanted a teacher who was going to be a good fit for the school, but their behavior was appalling.

As I drove home, I replayed the scene in my mind. I had come across many bullies in my life, especially on the soccer field, and I'd learned how to handle them by resisting my impulse to retaliate and moving on. But I remembered jump-kicking a kid in Long Beach when I was in second grade, fighting a fifth grader at recess when I was in fourth grade in Green Bay, and sucker-punching a kid who made me angry on the playground that same year. Now, of course, I was an adult with better self-control and more important things to focus on. I simply wanted to be a teacher, to make a difference for my students and society, and to support my family. But now I had witnessed the dark side of my profession.

Several weeks later, after much consideration, I decided I did not want to be in the same space as that administrator and his supporters. I returned to the job bidding fair and secured a different position at Einstein Middle School. Before I could leave, another man approached me. *Here we go again,* I thought to myself. But this interaction went quite differently.

"Hi," the man said, "I'm Gary. Congratulations. And welcome to Einstein Middle School. We look forward to having you next year. You'll be a great addition to an already great team." He sounded very sincere.

"Thank you," I responded. "I look forward to being there. I appreciate you welcoming me."

His warmth and dignity meant a lot to me.

The following year, I taught eighth grade language arts with three other teachers who all planned to retire at the end of the school year. Mr. Keefe, Mr. Demerath, and Mr. Benderling had been at Einstein for a long time. But with a year of teaching already under my belt, I seamlessly immersed myself into the culture at Einstein. I met many wonderful students, parents, and teachers, and I learned a great deal from them about life and my chosen career.

That spring of 2000, Maya and I became US citizens. I was entertaining the idea of one day joining the Peace Corps, and US citizenship was one of the application requirements. Though it provided us with a new sense of security, the process itself was a surprisingly straightforward and unemotional affair. Not long afterward, I again went to the job bidding fair. Although I loved the environment at Einstein, I wanted to see if I could get a position at a high school where I could also coach soccer—the reason I got into teaching in the first place. After the previous year's fiasco, I knew what to expect at the fair. This time, if anyone dared to push me around, I planned to simply brush them off. But there were no angry administrators this time around. I secured a position back at Appleton East High, where I would be teaching two American literature sections, two British literature sections, creative writing, and a course on contemporary American novels and short stories—all subjects I knew well and was excited to teach.

Perhaps even more exciting, before the end of the school year, I secured a coaching position on the East High freshmen soccer team for the upcoming fall season. Indeed, my dream was becoming a reality.

16

At East High School in the fall of 2000, I instantly felt welcome and right at home. Every day, I felt that I was learning, transforming, and becoming a better teacher and person. Due to my diligence in planning and preparation, I had no student disciplinary incidents. And I had a great time coaching the freshmen boys' soccer team, just as I had envisioned, using soccer to engage, inspire, and transform students. The first quarter passed quickly.

Then, a week before our winter break, I learned Vang was in the hospital. At first, I didn't think much of it because he had been hospitalized quite frequently in recent years. His doctors had warned him many times to cut down or completely stop his alcohol consumption. In fact, they nearly committed him to the hospital on several occasions. But he couldn't control his addiction.

My sister called the day before winter break and told me Vang had undergone surgery to remove a blood clot from his brain and that he was doing well. Again, since this type of hospitalization wasn't unusual for him, I wasn't worried. I told Yanghoua I would visit him after the kids and I were out of school.

When Maya and I finally drove to Green Bay to visit Vang on December 23, he was unresponsive. I didn't want to accept that he might never wake up. Many friends and community members visited, sharing their belief that he would be fine, which provided me with some much-needed comfort. It was almost midnight by the time we returned home.

The next day, Christmas Eve, we visited him again. When we arrived, his skin looked normal and the vitals on the machines remained unchanged. As we sat in the waiting room, we thought he could wake up at any moment. But within half an hour, everything changed. My sister-in-law came into the waiting room and announced that the doctor wanted to see me and the rest of the family. I wished so badly for good news. After we'd gathered in one of the private rooms, the doctor said, "I'm so sorry to tell you this, but your brother is no longer living. Your family will need to make some decisions."

The news hit me hard. I had been so hopeful, and I felt completely unprepared for this reality. I hugged my sister and cried like I never had. It wasn't the first time I had lost a family member, but I could no longer rely on my innocence to lessen the grief. Maya stood by my side, but she couldn't console me. I just sobbed and hugged my sister until my tears slowly subsided. With the exception of Vang's oldest daughter and son-in-law and Kong, who was away at college, all of our immediate family members were present. When Vang's daughter and son-in-law arrived, we all broke into tears all over again.

After a while, I recognized it was time for Vang to be given a haircut and a shave. I calmly accepted this unspoken duty. All of my siblings knew I should be the one to complete this task. Vue and Pheng were deeply affected by deaths they had witnessed and struggled to cope with it. Kong wasn't around. Yanghoua was married, which meant her soul and spirits were now aligned not with our family but with her husband's.

Everyone left the room, and I turned off the respirator. I then waited for the coroner to arrive and legally declare the time of death. Vang and I were two lonely souls, bonded by blood and brotherhood, going our separate ways. I now had just memories and stories of him left. I clenched his hand and spoke to him, expressing my gratitude for all that he had done for me.

> I still remember when you told me not to worry when I traveled, for you were watching and protecting me. Whenever

> I was away, I knew you were protecting me from dangers. You meant the world to me. I also want to apologize for not being able to help you. I'm so sorry I couldn't save you. When you go to Heaven and see Mom and Dad and the rest of our siblings, please tell them I'm doing well. Go in peace, my brother. It has been my honor to be your brother. I will see you soon.

I then gave him a haircut and shave as I waited for the coroner to arrive. I watched his skin change to a pale yellow and felt his hand stiffen and become cold.

My uncle thanked everyone for their support and encouraged us to head to Vang's house to keep the place warm and keep his family company. There, we didn't sleep at all. When morning came, Maya and I drove home to celebrate Christmas with our kids. Their innocence and excitement as they opened their gifts brought me solace and kept Vang's death from occupying my mind. Once this precious time with our kids was over, we drove back to Green Bay to discuss funeral arrangements with the family. Vang's funeral would be held on the first weekend after the New Year. I was scheduled to teach, but my principal kindly honored my request to take a five-day funeral leave.

Maya and I spent the week before the funeral visiting my sister-in-law, nieces, and nephews. Vang's youngest daughter wasn't even one year old. Many people, including family, relatives, and community members, visited their house and often stayed late into the night. Some of the men played cards and talked while some of the women prepared meals. Many family members cut and folded spiritual money into miniature canoes, which would be burned at the end of the funeral; these represented a form of wealth that Vang would carry with him into the spiritual world. We decorated several posters with pictures of Vang and his family and created an informational sheet listing highlights from his life.

Maya and I left our children at home with their grandmother while we traveled to Green Bay, and we often began our long drive back to Appleton around midnight. Fortunately, the weather was not as bad as it could have been.

As I participated in these activities throughout the week, I couldn't help but feel happy for Vang. By most people's standards, he probably didn't live the best life. His drinking certainly caused many problems. But those of us who were close to him appreciated his sincerity and generosity. Boom, Vang's brother-in-law from Long Beach, also came. It had been more than twenty years since we were kids playing around our apartment on Magnolia Avenue, Drake Park, and along the Los Angeles River. He wasn't the kid I remembered; he'd grown much taller and bigger, and he didn't remember me at all. I realized that some people we cross paths with may be important to us, though we may not be important to them, and that's okay.

When Friday finally came, I was relieved. I wanted the event to be over as soon as possible and to move on with my life. Early that morning, my sister-in-law and sister, as well as some other women, had gone to dress Vang's body at the Schauer and Schumacher funeral home on Monroe Avenue. It was important that the coffin, clothes, and items to be buried with him were nonmetallic, as metals would rust and could give Vang a terminal disease in his afterlife or reincarnation.

By late morning, Vang's body was transported to the Schauer and Schumacher funeral home on Fisk Street, near Colburn Park, where many Hmong used to play soccer in the 1980s. Hmong funerals are often held here because it's the only funeral home in the city that offers a twenty-four-hour service.

By the time the funeral started on Friday morning, I was already exhausted, physically and emotionally. I hadn't been sleeping well since Vang's death, and I was trying to support his family while also ensuring that the funeral went smoothly.

Vang's body rested on the floor in the middle of the room, and the women in our family were directed to sit by his side as the funeral proceeded. I've never enjoyed funerals. I hate the constant beating of the drums, the high and low pitches from the bamboo instrument qeej, and the sight of weeping guests and, especially, dead people. In the days since Vang's death, my mind had been flooded with faces of dead people I'd seen, including the person with the purple tongue I'd seen as a child in Laos, and of course my father. I do have a positive association with the funerals of my mother and sister, but that's because I didn't attend them.

A man sitting by Vang began the funeral by saying, "Vang, I see that you are dressed nicely today. Is this a special day for you? And are you going somewhere today? If it is a special day for you today and if you are going somewhere, please get up and go." He repeated these questions and statements many times. Receiving no response from Vang, the man continued, "If you are, then why are you lying there and why aren't you responding to my questions? Please tell me why you are dressed nicely and are you going somewhere today?"

After repeating these questions many times with no response from Vang, the man said, "Since you are not responding, please tell us whether you are dead or are you still alive? Please tell me. If you are alive, please get up and tell me, because this isn't a time for you to be lying there." The man repeated these statements and questions as well. Finally, exhausted from the repetition, the man said, "Since you are not responding, then you must be dead. If you are dead, is this why you are dressed so nicely, so that you can make your way to heaven? Again, I ask you, why are you dressed so nicely today? If you are planning to go somewhere special, get up now and go; otherwise, you are dead and are all dressed up to be on your way to heaven."

Several hours of this ritual passed until the man started shedding tears. His sorrow soon consumed the room. I began crying uncontrollably. Others tried to comfort me, but it didn't work. The pain was immense and intense, and it increased when I began thinking of my parents as well. Soon, my eyes hurt, and my body felt tight. Eventually, I ran out of tears and was able to gather myself.

Eventually, the man proceeded, "Since you are indeed dead, let me guide you to heaven. I ask that you don't take any possessions that don't belong to you. I ask that you leave behind your family, wife, friends, and everyone in this room and go as peacefully as you came to this world." After repeating this many times, a musician began playing the qeej tu siav or "end of life" song. I wasn't familiar with the song, but its sorrowful notes touched my soul and seemed to empty the oxygen from the room. Even the qeej player paused several times to wipe away his tears.

Vang's body was eventually placed in the coffin in the front of the room, signaling the next phase of the funeral. The atmosphere became calm and peaceful once again, and people went back to whatever it was they had been doing earlier—talking, playing cards, drinking, and socializing.

For the next two nights, my siblings and our families slept at the funeral home. The rituals began in the late morning and continued until about midnight. By two or three in the morning, our immediate family members were the only ones left in the funeral home. Each day, in the early morning around five or six, I was awoken by loud, sorrowful cries coming from people beside the open casket. People cried about those they had lost—parents, children, spouses, loved ones, and all kinds of relatives. People cried about hardships, loneliness, and tragedies. Some asked Vang to carry their messages to their loved ones in the spiritual world.

Around midnight on Sunday, we gathered around Vang's coffin and kneeled with a couple sticks of burning incense in our hands. In front of us stood a gentleman in his early fifties in a black suit, white shirt, black tie, and black hat. We had invited him to accompany Vang on his journey to heaven. As Vang's medium, he shared Vang's last messages with his family, friends, and community. Vang's messages to us were life lessons about morality: Don't cheat on your spouse, don't gamble your savings away, treat each other with love and respect, learn to be a just leader, don't be an alcoholic or womanizer, and many other pieces of advice.

The part that held the most meaning for me was toward the end when the man said, "Vang, your white horse has arrived. Get on it and be on your way to heaven. Don't look back, and don't bother anyone you left behind. Go on with your peace and leave them with their peace." Then the man addressed us: "Your husband, your dad, your brother, and your friend has left you. But don't cry. He has gone to heaven. He has gone on to a better place. In your time of need, I've found him a burial place made of gold and with white elephant teeth. If you want to visit him, go there." He wiped his tears, and the session was over.

We then prepared Vang for his burial. After burning the spiritual money, we followed the hearse and arrived at the cemetery where his grave awaited. One of my uncles conducted the necessary cultural steps to send Vang off, including the ritual of slashing the coffin a few times with a knife, symbolically cutting ties between Vang and the world of the living. The coffin was opened one last time, and we shed our last tears. Once the coffin was lowered into the ground, we covered it with shovels of dirt. I left the cemetery feeling conflicted. I was glad Vang had escaped his suffering, but he was leaving behind a family who would now suffer in his absence.

Over the course of the three-day funeral, I learned a lot. I'd asked the elders about the purpose of the funeral, the reason for its length, and to define the word *dab* or *monster*. It simply means "things we do not see or do not have the answers for."

After the burial, I visited my brother's grave several times. On his tombstone was a picture of him in Thailand, smiling with one foot on a soccer ball. Each time I saw it, happy memories replaced my thoughts of the hardships he had to endure. On one visit, I realized that at forty-two, Vang had lived to be older than any other member of our immediate family. I had heard the cliché that life is short, but I had never thought much about it until now. I was twenty-nine years old—thirteen years away from Vang's age at his death, twelve years away from my dad's age at his death, and eight years away from my mom's age at her death. *Everything is impermanent,* I thought, *and time is not merciful.* I reflected on this as I returned to my normal routine—teaching, playing soccer, doing chores, and spending time with Maya and our kids.

Amid these everyday tasks, I also worked on the final chapter of my dissertation, which explored Hmong students' journeys through college. I interviewed and recorded my participants throughout Wisconsin and a few in Minnesota, transcribing all the interviews, coding the data, and drafting the final chapter. Since my dissertation chair planned to be on sabbatical in spring 2002, I needed to get my dissertation completed and defend it before the end of the fall 2001 semester.

By the time of my graduation ceremony in December 2001, a year had passed since Vang's death. About thirty members of my family—including my brothers, cousins, nieces, nephews, and in-laws—traveled to Madison and stayed at the Crowne Plaza Hotel on East Washington Avenue. We all woke up early to take group pictures in the lobby before making our way to the Kohl Center, where I would be receiving my doctorate in educational administration.

Though I knew it was an important moment, I wasn't too excited. In some ways, earning my bachelor's degree had been a more impressive accomplishment. I had never cared for the music, crowds, and energy at these types of ceremonies. In

In the spring of 2001, a few of my Appleton East High School communication arts students wanted to take a picture with me (far left) for posterity.

particular, I found the tradition of doctoral graduates wearing elaborate caps and gowns to be rather silly. When the event was finally over, my family grabbed a meal at a local buffet, and then everyone headed home.

Earlier that week, I had emailed several professors to thank them for their support during my doctoral program. Each one congratulated me, but one responded with a memorable message. She told me that with my degree, I now had more responsibility, and I needed to take care to represent myself well in my speech and actions. Her words reminded me of lectures I'd heard from Hmong elders growing up. At the time, I couldn't fully grasp her words. Deep down, I knew I was like a tree with deep roots—I wouldn't suddenly change because of accolades or achievements.

I finished the school year at East with my doctorate and planned to return the following year. After four years of teaching,

I'd finally found my dream job, and I was making a difference in my students' lives. I'd convinced Bobby to set his sights on owning a repair shop, rather than simply being a car repairman, because one day the physical work would catch up with him. I learned from students like Matthew and Matt not to stifle teens who had alternative interests but instead to let their creativity, curiosity, and imagination guide their learning. And it really lifted my spirits when one of my retiring colleagues told me, "You're a great teacher and human being. One day, you will become a legendary teacher at Appleton East High School." I smiled and contained my enthusiasm in front of him, but inside, I was honored and overjoyed by his comment. He gifted me a framed purplish Hmong paj ntaub, or decorative cloth, which I still have.

17

A week after school ended in the summer of 2002, I became restless. My UW–Oshkosh professor Dr. Lampe had given me some advice after my graduation: "Earn your job, study your job, learn your job, know your job, perform your job, and then move on. That's how you will grow and impact the profession. Plus, life's too short. Go and live life." I was inspired. I updated my resume and cover letter and applied to several associate principal positions, mainly to test Dr. Lampe's advice. Nobody called, but part of me felt relieved. I wasn't so sure what I would do if someone did.

Then one day, to my great surprise, a representative from the Green Bay Area Schools called. The next thing I knew, I was in my old neighborhood interviewing for an administrative position. The district's office was about two miles from the first house where I'd lived in Green Bay. A mile away was Seymour Park, where I used to play marbles for money to ensure that Kong and I had our breakfast. I thought about what my younger self would think if he could see me now.

When I walked in, I felt immediately intimidated by the large square table with principals sitting around it. The scene reminded me of one from stories of King Arthur and his knights of the Round Table. After taking my seat on the empty side of the table, I took a deep breath. I was nervous, but I became more confident with each question they asked me, and my anxiety soon vanished. I told them my priority as a school administrator would be safety—if people don't feel safe, they can't learn. In addition to physical safety, I would work to establish safety from social injustices, safety from prejudice, safety from discrimination, and safety from undue stress. A few days later, they contacted me for a second interview.

This time, I was interviewed by the superintendent, Dan Nerad, and assistant superintendent, David Zadnik. I felt very comfortable in their presence. After the pleasantries, Dan said, "Well, you did well in the interview. We were most impressed, and we would like to offer you an associate principal position with the school district. You would work half-time at Edison Middle School and half-time at East. You would serve as associate principal and activities director for each school."

When he told me the salary for the position, I almost went into cardiac arrest. It was a considerable increase from my previous teaching salaries. I told them I appreciated the opportunity and that I would let them know my decision by Monday.

That weekend, I coached my youth soccer team at Neenah Memorial Park. After one of our games, I ran into David Zadnik in the parking lot. His son was also playing in the tournament. "Okay, Pao," he said, smiling. "We don't have to wait until Monday."

"Sounds good, David," I told him. "I'm in."

We shook hands.

As I prepared for this new adventure in my work life, I was also presented with an exciting opportunity in my athletic life. A week before my first day as an administrator, one of my uncles invited me to join him at a Labor Day soccer tournament in Green Bay. His team, the Black Cats, needed a defensive central midfielder. I happily agreed, as the Black Cats were known for their incredible talent. Some players had a history of exhibiting volatile behaviors on the field, yet they did not have a reputation as a violent team. Over the last decade, Hmong soccer tournaments had become hubs for intimidation and violence. Some Hmong gangs had even chosen soccer tournaments as their battlefields. These environments had become so hostile that some soccer players had chosen to abandon the game altogether. Playing with the Black Cats, I knew I wouldn't have to worry about being targeted or retaliated against on or off the field.

I also agreed to play because even though I was thirty, I knew I could still play at a high level. My passion and competitive spirit hadn't waned a bit since I first stepped onto the soccer field in 1985. Ever since I was seventeen, I had been a free agent, meaning I had never committed to playing on a particular team. As a free agent, I had to prove myself to the players, coaches, and managers every time I stepped onto the field. For many years, I had been running in the mornings, doing drills and lifting weights in the afternoons, and scrimmaging in the evenings. As I aged and suffered a handful of injuries, I worked diligently to rely less on my speed and to become a more strategic, intellectual player. I also learned to adapt my playing style depending on the team, coach, and opponents. In other words, I had stopped playing soccer and instead I had become a part of it.

When Labor Day weekend came, I was ready to prove my worth. In each of the first two games, the coach put me in when we were ahead for the last twenty minutes of the game. After the coach had announced the lineup for our third game, one of the players interrupted him and suggested I start in the number six position. In soccer, the number six can do it all—defend, pass, dribble, shoot, and run up and down the field. I took this as a great compliment. During the prior two games, this player had noticed that I made the game easier for the team when I was on the field. Because this player was our main attacking midfielder and most gifted player, the coach took his suggestion and put me in.

We won our next two games, but sadly, we lost the finals in a shootout. I missed my penalty kick. Fortunately, my overall performance was strong enough that they invited me back to the team. I would go on to play with the Black Cats for the next five years until an injury forced my departure. During those five years, I never missed another penalty kick.

I started my new job—spending mornings at Edison Middle School and afternoons at East High—with the motivation to learn new skills and master them. At East, it felt surreal to be working with my former chemistry teacher, who was now one of the associate principals, and also to be evaluating some of my former teachers.

The demographics at East had gone from being predominantly Caucasian when I was a student to being predominantly non-white, with a large Latino student population. The building included a new gym, science wing, and multiple parking lots. The school had also built a new stadium. In fact, the newly renovated stadium now reminded me of the old City Stadium at East, where the Packers had played for decades before moving to Lambeau Field. Much of the refurbished brick flooring from the old City Stadium was kept as a tribute to Curly Lambeau and Vince Lombardi. I was surprised by the surveillance cameras in the hallways and on the school's exterior. Also, as an administrator, I was more aware of student truancy, students' various mental health issues, and the fights and scuffles that took place, including a melee in the cafeteria that was sensationalized by local news outlets for a few days.

At Edison, the students were still predominantly Caucasian, with a growing Latino student population. It surprised me to learn that gangs were more of an issue at Edison than at East. Some students, lacking the necessary academic, social, and emotional skills to succeed in middle school, took such inadequacies to mean that they were unintelligent and that they had no hope of succeeding in the future. I often had to remind them that they still had the potential to achieve something great. Building trust and positive relationships with students—as well as teachers, parents, staff, and community members—was at the core of my administrative approach.

Once that spring, as I was leaving a meeting with several other administrators, I overheard someone ask, "How do we know if Pao even has a doctorate? He could have just framed a certificate and hung it on the wall." I was shocked, but I decided there was nothing I could do other than continue to co-exist with this person in a professional context.

After a year at East and Edison, I was feeling quite confident in my job. I fully expected to keep it for at least several more years. But then one day, I added up the amount of time I was spending on the road. Two hours a day, five days a week, for forty-eight weeks per year equaled four hundred and eighty hours a year. I was spending nearly a month of each year on the road.

Thinking about my former dissertation adviser's advice to keep moving on to new challenges, I began browsing a website listing Wisconsin school administrator positions. I soon found an opening at Neenah High School, which was much closer to my home and would offer me a set of new challenges. I applied, and a few days later I got a call.

It was a typical sunny and hot June day when I arrived for my interview at the Neenah Joint School District building. Its large hallway and high ceiling made me feel like I was in a mansion or small cathedral. The room was intimidating, with six or seven people around a horseshoe-shaped table asking me questions. I felt like I was being interrogated in a court room. As in my Green Bay interview, I felt calm and confident throughout the process, but this time, the interview seemed to last for hours. Also, it was followed by a memorable interaction.

After I walked out of that interview session, I was greeted by Mark Duerwaechter, the Neenah High School principal. He was tall and sharply dressed. He led me outside and into the passenger seat of his Ford Taurus. As he began driving to Neenah High

School, he said, "So, Pao, tell me, if you could do anything for a living, and I mean anything, what would you do? Be honest." I felt comfortable with Mark, even though we had only met ten minutes earlier. Somehow, I felt like we had known each other for a long time.

"Hmm," I thought. "I would love to write and travel for a living." This was the first thing that came to my mind, even though writing is a challenge for me, as a non-native English speaker.

"Why?" Mark asked.

"I just want freedom," I answered. "I could write on the beach. On a plane. At midnight. Two in the morning. Whenever. Wherever. On whatever topics."

"That's great," he said. "Now tell me, before you try to do that, how many years do think you could commit to this position?"

"At least two years," I told him. A friend had recently advised me to try a job for two to three years and then go on from there. If a job simply isn't a good fit, though, one year would be enough. It isn't worth sacrificing one's spirit, emotions, and well-being to get to the two- or three-year mark.

Later that week, they called and offered me the job. Starting in July 2003, I would be at Neenah High School. I would miss working with the wonderful teachers and students at East and Edison, though I would not miss the administrative colleague who had made that rude comment. One parting gift from a teacher at East captured what I had learned from my time in all of my teaching positions so far. It was a magnet with the words, "Peace. It does not mean to be in a place where there is no noise, trouble, or hard work. It means to be in the midst of those things and still be calm in your heart."

18

Starting the job at Neenah High School in the summer of 2003 was challenging. I was in the middle of teaching a precollege summer course at UW–Oshkosh and completing a school finance course at Marian College to get my principal license. I decided I would spend my first two months on the job focusing on two major tasks: coordinating and managing the summer school program and strategizing for the upcoming year. I had more than fifty teachers and staff members to supervise, manage, and evaluate. I also added student management to my strategic plan, as I wanted to ensure that my practices aligned with the norms at Neenah High School and the policies set by the Board of Education, including detentions, suspensions, and expulsions. I focused on these areas because they involved building relationships and trust.

In August, I attended several district meetings and gatherings and got to know the district administrative team. Because the Neenah Joint School District is a relatively small school district, I quickly immersed myself in its culture, from the building administrators to the district administrators, and from the school board to the community.

A few months after the school year started, I quickly learned why Neenah High School needed six administrators. With more than two thousand students and more than two hundred teachers, staff, and volunteers, a small team of professionals was needed to handle student management, the school curriculum and policies, athletics and co-curricular activities, public relations, and teacher and staff support. Throughout each day, in one form or another, these topics all came into play. The only constant amid the chaos was that we all worked diligently to create a culture and climate that could inform and transform individuals. And we worked hard to minimize any threats that could jeopardize such harmony.

In December, Maya and I attended a Christmas gathering at Mark Duerwaechter's house. Maya, pregnant with our fourth child due that August, was distracted, but I had one of the best times of my life. It had been a while since I had felt so in sync with my coworkers. The gathering infused me with an energy that boosted me through the harsh winter months.

Before long, it was spring. The seniors began to prepare for graduation, with summer just around the corner. At the end of one day, I checked my email and one caught my attention. It was from Neenah High School's Talented and Gifted coordinator. She'd sent me information about a Fulbright-Hays Study Abroad Project to go to Thailand and Laos. I discovered the project was being sponsored by the Wisconsin Department of Public Instruction. In the nearly twenty-five years since I'd left Southeast Asia to come to the United States, I hadn't thought about returning to Thailand or Laos. The application was long, and it was due in about two weeks. I looked at the number of questions and was quickly overwhelmed. But with Maya's encouragement, in the ensuing days, I completed the application and sent it out, not expecting much in return.

A couple weeks later, I had one of my most memorable interactions with a parent in my time as an administrator. A very angry father visited my office to talk about how I had suspended his daughter, Beth, for fighting the previous day. Beth, a first-year student, often wore army pants with a white tank top and carried a well-loved teddy bear around school with her. As I understood it, she had grabbed another student by the neck, kneed him, and threw him against the wall because she had seen him spit on another student's face.

After a teacher who witnessed the episode brought the two

students to my office, I listened to Beth tell her side of the story. She was cooperative and calmly shared her justification for her actions. The other student confirmed Beth's version of events. Typically, a fight like this would result in an automatic five-day out-of-school suspension, but in this case, I suspended both Beth and the other student for three days. I couldn't help remembering how an administrator had simply sent me back to class after I'd been caught fighting a kid in my eighth grade gym class.

Beth's father arrived at the main office around ten o'clock the next morning. The office assistant warned me that he was on his way to my office. She told me, with some humor, "He's a big, rugged guy, Pao. And he looks very angry." I'd dealt with similar experiences before, and I wasn't disturbed. But as a precaution, I told my assistant, Maggie, "When Mr. Brown gets here, let him in, and don't try to stop him."

"Do you want me to keep the door open?" she asked.

"Yes, that would be great. Also, have the radio ready for Officer Pat."

Within a few minutes, Mr. Brown walked through the door, breathing heavily. He was about five-foot-ten and at least two hundred and fifty pounds with a beer belly. He hadn't shaved for a while, and his unbuttoned brown coat had a few dark stains on the front.

"I want to see the videos now," he demanded in a deep voice.

"Mr. Brown, please take a seat and we can talk about it," I said politely, guiding him to a chair with my open palm. He remained standing. "Please, Mr. Brown." Again, I gestured for him to sit. Within a minute, he regained his breath, his face became less red, and he took a seat. "Now," I proceeded. "What questions or concerns do you have?"

"I want to see the videos," he demanded.

"I'm going to be honest with you, Mr. Brown," I said. "There's no video."

"Beth told me you threatened her. She said you had a video of her beating that boy." He was still heated.

"Oh that, we do that all the time," I assured him. "We have a few cameras in the hallway. I told her to tell me the truth, so that I don't have to go and look at the video. That was all."

"Is there a video?" he asked.

"No, there's no video," I repeated. "Do you want to know what happened?" By this point, he had calmed quite a bit.

"Yes," he said.

"I'm really glad Beth stood up for that boy yesterday," I told him. "I would have done the same. She was clearly angry after seeing what happened, but she didn't have to use force. It seems that she left a scar on the boy's neck, but his parents didn't file any charges, given his bad behavior as well." Mr. Brown listened attentively as I finished the story. "Now, do you still have any questions for me?" I asked him. The anger and frustration on his face had now vanished, and he seemed to understand that I wasn't out to get his daughter.

"No." With that response, I thought he'd stand up, shake my hand, and leave. But there was a long pause. Then, unexpectedly, he blurted out, "Life has been difficult for me." Suddenly, he started sobbing. "I just got out of jail and got custody of Beth. Her mom ran away and abandoned her. And I don't want to do the same thing to her that I did to her older sister." Through his sobs, he continued to share his life story. He was an alcoholic and a drug user, and he had molested his older daughter. I offered him the tissue box.

"One morning," he explained, "around two in the morning, after drinking a lot, I went and stood in the middle of the road, hoping to be run over. But I fell asleep. And when I woke up, there were no cars. I was still alive. I didn't die. I didn't get run over. And that's when I knew I was being punished. So, I went to the sheriff and turned myself in. Since then, I've accepted God, and I'm trying really, really hard to put my life back together."

I, of course, wasn't expecting this. He needed someone to talk to, and I happened to be the one. We talked for an additional five or so minutes before he was comfortable enough to leave. After this stunning interaction, I returned to my office, took off my sport coat, released my necktie, and sank into my office chair. I stretched out my legs, planted my heels on top of the desk, and took a deep breath. I then did my daily ritual, reminding myself that as terrible as some of my days may be, even my worst concerns are small compared to those of some of the people who walk into my office.

It had been a long day, but before heading home, I realized I had received a letter from the Wisconsin DPI. I opened the envelope immediately. Inside, the letter read, "Congratulations on being selected as a recipient for the Wisconsin Department of Public Instruction Fulbright-Hays Project: Highlighting Southeast Asian Cultures and Heritage."

I paused, then exhaled slowly. After twenty-seven years, I was going home.

To prepare for the two-month study abroad, I attended several DPI seminars at UW–Milwaukee. Eighteen of us, from a variety of backgrounds, would be participating. I was grateful that the Neenah Joint School District agreed to accommodate my leave.

When June came around, Maya and the kids dropped me off at Mitchell International Airport in Milwaukee, where we'd found the cheapest flights. After I waved goodbye, I wouldn't see them again for almost two months. First, I flew to Chicago, where I met up with a few other participants. Then, we had a long flight from Chicago to Tokyo. In Japan, we met up with more participants, some of whom had flown out of Detroit. The two-hour rest at Tokyo Airport was much needed. For the first time in years, I was surrounded by Asian people, yet I felt so out of touch and out of place.

On my final flight to Bangkok, I felt completely inundated with Asian culture. It was surreal to hear Japanese and Thai announcements over the speakers, though I had no idea what was being said. My brain overflowed with internal conflicts, but this sense of not belonging with any particular group wasn't new to me. Over the course of my life, I had grown quite accustomed to it. In fact, I had come to embrace it. As I processed my thoughts on the plane to Thailand, I told myself over and over, *It's okay to be different.*

19

Around one in the morning, we landed in Bangkok at Don Muang International Airport. In the 1970s, 1980s, and 1990s, many Hmong refugees departed from Don Muang on their way to France, Australia, Canada, and the United States. My siblings and I were among them.

Once we stepped outside the airport, I was instantly soaked by the humidity. I couldn't remember experiencing anything like it. I couldn't wait until I got into one of the air-conditioned vans. As we coasted along the highway, I was mesmerized by Bangkok's skyline and so grateful for this opportunity to return home. I silently expressed my thanks to the individuals who made this project possible, including the late Senator J. William Fulbright.

When we stopped at a restaurant before heading to our hotel, the ambience brought a flood of memories back. I remembered the heat and humidity, the fans blowing, the smells of authentic Thai food mixed with other less pleasant odors, the moldy concrete buildings, the electrical wires hanging everywhere, the sky covered with gray smoke, and Thai people everywhere I looked. I felt such a strong sense of belonging, while also feeling like a stranger.

For the next two weeks, our group of eighteen Fulbright participants remained in Bangkok. We met with many school and governmental officials and visited schools, historical sites, and shopping areas—places I never would have been able to access had my family remained in Thailand or Laos.

During our final weekend in Bangkok, another scholar and I stayed in the home of a local Thai teacher of Chinese ancestry.

First, he brought us to visit the school where he taught, Suankularb Wittayalai, one of the biggest and most prestigious boys' high schools in the city. Our host shared that many Thai prime ministers had attended this school in their youth. During the school's morning assembly, we stood on a stage with the principal before thousands of students who stood in neat lines in their uniforms, almost like soldiers. I shared a bit of myself, including my years living in Thailand and my happiness to return to this place that felt like home. Later, our host took us to Kanchanaburi Province where we visited the River Kwai and the Kanchanaburi War Cemetery. There, we saw graves of British, Australian, and Dutch prisoners of war who had died after being imprisoned by the Japanese and forced to build the Burma Railway.

After the group reconvened, we shared our experiences staying with different Thai host teachers. Some stayed in beautiful houses in the city and explored various neighborhoods and historical sites, some stayed in the countryside and got a good taste of Thai rural life, and some stayed in beach houses near the ocean where they got to examine Thai fisheries and local seafood eateries.

After Bangkok, we headed north to Chiang Mai, Thailand, by coach. On the way, we visited Wat Tham Krabok, a refugee camp on the grounds of a Buddhist monastery where many Hmong had lived since the mid-1990s when Ban Vinai Refugee Camp in Loei had closed. At one time, more than thirty thousand Hmong lived here, mainly those whose parents had fled from Laos to Thailand in the 1970s and 1980s and had decided against relocating abroad. About a year earlier, in 2003, the United States had granted permission for the Hmong residing in Wat Tham Krabok to immigrate. We were educated about the Hmong who planned to relocate in the hopes that we might work with school districts and communities when we returned to the United States to prepare for their arrival.

During our visit, we met with the Thai authorities overseeing and managing Wat Tham Krabok, including Colonel Paradorn, who gave a presentation about the Hmong and other groups living there. I learned that Wat Tham Krabok wasn't recognized as an official refugee camp, which meant it had no support from international organizations and, as a result, the people living there had no proper sewage system, running water, or medical services.

We met an African American monk who had grown up in New York, fought in Vietnam, and never left. We also met with local Hmong leaders, who shared about life in the Wat and how the immigration process was coming along for families planning to relocate to the United States. On a tour, we learned about the different ban or divisions within the camp, and their leaders. The sights, sounds, and ways of life in the camp made me feel like I was hallucinating. I was reminded of my time in Ban Nong Khai and Ban Vinai, when I experienced so much uncertainty and hopelessness.

The next day, we visited Ban Tharn Thong Daeng School, a Thai school located near Wat Tham Krabok. Hmong families who had the financial means sent their children to this school. The curriculum was somewhat similar to a typical US curriculum, with required core classes and electives. But the Thai school used more structured instructional approaches, and the students had fewer resources and very limited, if any, post-secondary opportunities. The teachers also shared that many Hmong students had stopped attending since their families had learned of their potential relocation to the United States.

After a brief tour of the school, we headed back to Wat Tham Krabok, where we were paired with Hmong students who showed us around. At the Hmong school inside the camp, we saw first-grade students learning the alphabet and a group of middle school students learning English, which had become part of the curriculum after news of the relocation was received. Some of the

When I visited the Wat Tham Krabok refugee camp in Thailand in 2004, I took many photographs to document the people and conditions there, including this one of children, adults, and typical dwellings inside the camp. THE SOUTHEAST ASIAN IMAGES AND TEXTS PROJECT, UNIVERSITY OF WISCONSIN-MADISON ARCHIVES

teachers were as young as fifteen or sixteen years old. For the most part, the classrooms were dirty. The students sat at long tables and benches, rather than desks. Yet, despite the conditions and limited resources, there was no doubt about the students' passion to learn.

As we toured the rest of Wat Tham Krabok, I noticed small shelters made of concrete or wood with sheet metal roofs. I spoke with some residents, who told me conditions in the Wat hadn't changed much since they'd first arrived, but there had been many positive improvements, such as stores, a post office, computers, televisions, cell phones, cars, and other motor vehicles. Many residents could afford various forms of technology, even though the infrastructure was not set up to support things like a sewage system or running water. A few asked me whether life in the United States was as good as people had told them. My response was, "I can tell you that life isn't going to be any easier, but America gives you the opportunity to move and change your life, if you are willing to work hard." They seemed glad to hear my candid response.

Later, two elderly women asked me a similar question. This time, I respectfully told them, "Life isn't easy anywhere in the world, but I know that if you stay here, your hopes and dreams will die here. If you go to America, your hopes and dreams will live on and may one day be fulfilled by your grandchildren and great-grandchildren." They smiled. I smiled and told them, "I'll see you in America."

As we made our way out of the camp, I came across a Hmong American man who was volunteering there. He told me, "Take lots and lots of pictures. They will be the true stories of this place." And I did. I photographed the cemetery, barbed wire fences, small businesses, children and elders, the open sewage system, and other aspects of life inside Wat Tham Krabok.

In Chiang Mai, we stayed at a hotel near the Night Bazaar. After settling in our hotel, I was glad to find a nearby cleaning place where I could have my laundry done. The cost was reasonable, yet I still felt conflicted—I thought my laundry should be something I did myself.

We visited many schools in Chiang Mai, including one where tribal students from the surrounding rural areas attended. Over 50 percent of the students were Hmong. The students lived at the school, and many visited their villages just a few times a year, typically during New Year. Since this school prepared students for jobs, most of them would not have an opportunity for higher education. A few could still speak Hmong, but most couldn't, having left their villages as young children. We also met a Hmong researcher at Chiang Mai University, and he provided us with statistics and information about the Hmong in Thailand. Visiting many local markets opened our eyes to how people there made a living. I was overwhelmed with all of the new information and experiences. I wasn't sure about the other Fulbright participants, but I wasn't too interested in the details; instead, I tried to transcend the details and soak in the essence of the place.

While my time in Chiang Mai was almost completely positive, I had a disappointing experience at a tribal museum. There, we watched a video on the many ethnic groups in Thailand, including the Hmong. The video showed a Hmong family conducting a ceremony and sacrificing a cat. They wrapped a rope around the cat's neck and led it around a fire. A shaman followed the cat, then drank some oil, blew it near the cat's back, and lit it on fire, catching part of the cat. He did this repeatedly, and the cat screeched and jumped in the air each time. I was greatly disturbed and unsettled. I had never seen or heard of anything like that. Perhaps this dark ceremony was an extreme religious interpretation of a traditional practice, but it certainly wasn't an accurate or fair depiction of Hmong cultural practices.

After Chiang Mai, we took a long bus trip east to Nong Khai, near the border of Laos. The roads passed through some of Thailand's most beautiful forests and reminded me of my early days in Laos. As we approached the city of Loei, someone commented that the Ban Vinai Refugee Camp was just over the nearby mountains. I was flooded with emotions and memories, but I sat quietly for the rest of the way. I wasn't in the spirit to engage in such a painful topic.

That night in my hotel room, I woke up from a dead sleep, looked at my sleeping roommate, and asked him, "Who are you? Who are you? And why are you here?" Eventually, he woke up and looked at me in confusion. I regained my senses, told my roommate I didn't know what had just transpired, and went back to sleep.

The next morning, I asked my roommate what he thought about it. He sarcastically replied, "You're strange, Pao. You're very strange, indeed. You must have had a traumatic childhood or something." I nodded in agreement and said nothing. But I thought, *I don't know if you would even believe me if I told you.* We visited an archeological site that day, but I found it hard to concentrate. Here, near the Mekong River, I had other things on my mind. I was born and raised not too far away, and my mother and sister had drowned near this place.

I knew the next day would be emotional for me, as we were heading to Laos. After our visas had been stamped and we crossed the Friendship Bridge over the Mekong River, I tuned out reality. I closed my eyes and paid my respects to my mom and sister. *I'm back, Mom, Dad, and sister Shoua,* I thought. That was as far as I got. If I continued, I would have been a mess, and my colleagues would have asked why.

The contrast between Thailand and Laos was instantly noticeable. Thailand was well-organized, while Laos was in disarray. The differences were apparent in everything from the rice plantations to the roads to the buildings. My next big test would be coming face to face with communism and its ideologies and politics, which I had been told about many times over the last two decades.

In our hotel, my roommate and I were shocked by the number of geckos inside our room. They were everywhere and made themselves right at home, even on the ceiling and in the bathroom. Since there was no breakfast at our hotel, the next morning, we moved to another hotel. We checked in early enough to have breakfast. When my roommate and I entered our room, we noticed that it looked as if it hadn't been renovated since it was built. The decor was from the 1960s and 1970s, with many tiles missing on the floor and in the bathroom. The only modern technology was an air conditioning unit hanging above the patio door.

While in the capital city of Vientiane, we visited the local university and the US embassy and had several formal meetings with the local Laotian government, including the governor, who flew in from a conference in southern Laos just to meet with us. All the while, though we were just two or three hundred miles from where I was born and raised, I didn't feel like I was home or even near home. The city life of Vientiane was vastly different from the world I grew up in. *Where are the mountains, valleys, mists, villages, and Hmong people?* I thought.

Soon, we were boarding our flight to Luang Prabang. We had initially planned to take a bus, but then we were told it was still too dangerous for a group like ours to be traveling on the ground. Through the plane window, I watched as we flew west over the Mekong River into Thailand, then headed north, crossing back into Laos. Luang Prabang looked beautiful with its red-roofed and white-walled buildings, its dirt roads and temples. Surrounding the city were lush forests that seem to go on forever.

We stayed in a hotel that resembled a French chateau. It had once been a summer getaway for the king and his family. This information thrilled some of my companions, but I was not much of a royalty enthusiast. In the distance, I could see rice plantations, palm trees, and the shapes of many mountains against the sky. In the ensuing days, we visited several schools, the governor's mansion, the mansion of the former king, various temples, and a few local villages. At the former king's palace, we saw artifacts from the 1950s and 1960s, including a picture of President John F. Kennedy and a room decorated by a Japanese artist using small ceramic pieces.

On our last day, without the knowledge of our accompanying Laotian government officials, we privately arranged for a boat to take us up the Mekong River to visit a village where moonshine was made, a cave, and some other small villages. On the way, the sight of logs floating down the brownish and murky river triggered memories of my mom, my sister, and others who had perished there. I didn't interact with my colleagues for the majority of the trip, but my daze was briefly interrupted when we came across kids swimming near the shore, jumping off rocks, and horsing around. We stopped at the Pak Ou Caves, filled with thousands of statues of Buddha. At the moonshine village, some of us tried the local moonshine, which was incredibly strong. At a restaurant overlooking the river, I enjoyed a beer with assistant superintendent (and future Wisconsin governor) Tony Evers, and we briefly talked about our school experiences at UW–Madison.

Over the next few days, I continued to have enriching experiences in Laos, shopping at the morning market, touring the streets of Vientiane by scooter, and getting a haircut at a local barbershop. Being engaged in the local Laotian culture reminded me of my brother Vang, who lived here before he crossed the Mekong River to get to Nong Khai with a cousin and a brother-in-law.

On our last night in Vientiane, we ate dinner at the Lan Xang Hotel with many local government officials. Afterward, I went to bed early. I had something that I needed to do because I wasn't sure if I would ever set foot in Laos again. That morning, I left the hotel before breakfast. As usual, it was sunny and humid. I waved to a tuk tuk driver. By this point, I had picked up a few Laotian and Thai phrases, and I told him to take me to the morning market. After buying some flowers, I asked the driver to take me to an area where I would have access to the Mekong River. I didn't have to say much. He understood what I wanted to do. He took me to an area with tall grasses and a clear path to the shore.

Facing the Mekong River as I had more than twenty-seven years ago, I composed myself and said,

> Mom and Shoua, I am your son Pao and your brother Touger. I've returned. I want you, Shoua, and Dad to know that I've made it, and I'm okay. Mom, all your children are okay, all growing up, and now living in America. I've come back to

> see all of you, perhaps for the last time, just like the time you visited me in my dream in Nong Khai. Again, I want you to know that all your children survived and are doing well. I've gone on and made something of myself. I hope you're looking down on me and are proud of me. You gave me a gift. You emptied my heart and filled it with sorrow, and ever since then, I've been filling it—with happiness and joy, and at times sadness. The world took all of you away from me and that poisoned my spirit, but all is good and okay. Because I've come to cure such poison with compassion and empathy.

I then imagined the four of us crying together and hugging one another.

With a heavy burden finally lifted from my spirit, I placed the flowers in the river and let them drift off. As they floated away, I imagined my family's life in heaven being just as beautiful as the scene in front of me. Before walking away from the Mekong River, perhaps for the last time, I paid a silent homage, *To everyone else who perished here, I wish you peace. May heaven look favorably upon you and all your loved ones who have survived. May you know that your sacrifices weren't forgotten.*

Sitting in the tuk tuk on my way back to the hotel, I thought about my life. If my parents had chosen to stay in the jungles and fight against the communists, I would have stayed with them. I thought about what Laos had taken away from me—my father, my mother, my sister, my innocence, and my sophisticated, ancient, tribal ways of life. I then thought about what Laos had given me—the strength to survive and the determination to succeed in this unpredictable, cruel, and beautiful world. Finally, I thought about Laos itself—its corruptions and ugliness, its eclectic cultures and natural beauty, its tribal history and modernized ideals, full of paradoxes, like life itself.

When I returned to the hotel, I felt renewed. I had faced my

At the farewell dinner of my 2004 Fulbright-Hays Study Abroad trip, I discovered a connection with two other UW–Madison alumni at my table: the Secretary of Education of Thailand and Wisconsin DPI assistant superintendent Tony Evers. While they had been protesting the wars in Southeast Asia in the 1960s and 1970s, I was trying to survive them.

horrific and tragic past, and it had changed me for the better. I now felt I could begin to welcome it back and embrace it again.

It was a long flight from Vientiane to Pattaya, Thailand, and then another lengthy drive the next day from Pattaya to Bangkok. Many scenes along the way stirred up memories of my time as a refugee, but what had recently seemed like a mysterious and distant world to me wasn't so mysterious or distant anymore.

PART IV

The Nest

Whatever comes from the brain carries the hue of the place it came from, and whatever comes from the heart carries the heat and color of its birthplace.

—Oliver Wendell Holmes Sr.

20

"Pao, it's the best job in the world," said the dean of professional studies at UW–Green Bay. "You just have to teach your classes and attend meetings. And then after that, you're on your own. It's as close to professional freedom as you can get. You can research whatever topics you like and even travel the world."

I didn't need any more convincing, though I was taking a significant pay cut. "Yes, let's make it happen," I told him.

My gift for the holidays was a new job and career. In nine months, in August 2005, I would start as an assistant professor of education at the University of Wisconsin–Green Bay. As in the past, I had very little idea what I had gotten myself into. I had limited knowledge of what it meant to be in a tenure-track faculty position, including the scholarship, teaching, and service needed to be tenured and promoted.

This next chapter in my life had gotten its start back in August 2004 when our fourth child, Reeve, was born. I took several weeks off to be with Maya. One day, we were visiting Maya's mom at 302 Welhouse Drive in Kimberly and were taking our usual walk with all four children to Sunset Park when we saw that a nearby house was for sale by owner. We grabbed a flyer, called the owners, and arranged to see it. We loved it. Plus, it was close to Maya's mom, who was helping us babysit Reeve. By October, we had officially moved in.

That fall, the new baby and new house were both giving me reason to reflect on my career. Heading into my second year at Neenah High School and my third year in administration, I knew that if I were to commit to a preK-12 administrative career,

I would want to position myself to become a principal, director of secondary education, director of instruction, assistant superintendent, and then potentially a superintendent. The more I pondered these various professional scenarios, the less interested I was in this particular career path. It would provide me almost no opportunity to expand my aspirations beyond the school district. I decided I would rather venture into the unknown than continue to pursue what was known but unfulfilling to me. I started to keep an eye out for what could be my next adventure. Then, one October morning, I came across the posting of a tenure-track assistant professor position in the Professional Program in Education at the University of Wisconsin–Green Bay. I skimmed the job description and qualifications, and they matched well with my experiences and credentials. Though the salary wasn't what I had expected, I thought it could be just the opportunity I was looking for.

About two weeks after an intimidating all-day campus interview, an offer, and a salary negotiation, I accepted the position. One thing factoring heavily into my decision was Reeve. Since his birth, I had been leaving home before he woke up and returning home after he'd already fallen asleep. I worried that he didn't even recognize me. Plus, my mother-in-law was aging, and I didn't want her to spend so much time babysitting Reeve. Of course, my salary was still very important. But I felt the new job would provide me with the career change I desired. A conversation with a colleague also helped. When asked about his career objectives, he told me, "My father was a teacher. My mother was a teacher. Teaching and administration are all I know. So, I don't think I'm going anywhere."

"I'm happy for you," I replied. "At least you know what you're doing and where you're heading. That must be a good feeling."

"I guess," he said. His plan involved several more years as an assistant administrator, perhaps a decade as a building administrator, and then a few years at central administration to cap things off before his retirement. But I could sense the resignation in his voice as he laid out this trajectory.

"It's a great plan," I said, trying to be encouraging. "I'm so glad that some of my former administrators and teachers didn't make many career moves. Any time I needed them, I knew where to find them." Yet, in that moment, I became even more determined to avoid reaching a point of boredom in my career and to strive to seek growth in my professional journey. While staying in one place might be good for some people, it was not what I wanted for myself.

It was difficult to tell Mark Duerwaechter that I was leaving. But he validated my decision, saying that I had fulfilled my obligation to stay for two years. He also said he had observed a change in me after my Fulbright-Hays Study Abroad experience, and he knew the scope of what I wanted to do with my career had gone beyond the borders of the Neenah Joint School District. Before I left his office, he said, "Pao, sometimes in life, God has a plan for each of us. And this is your plan." In all of the many conversations I'd had with Mark, this was the first time he mentioned God. His comment reminded me of a story I'd been told about how I'd miraculously survived a truck accident with my mom when I was just a few months old. *Perhaps,* I thought. *Perhaps there is a plan for me.*

Four years later, in August 2008, I was heading into my fourth fall semester at UW–Green Bay. The excitement and challenges of this new endeavor caused the time to pass rather quickly.

Ever since Maya's mom had moved to Sacramento to live with Maya's brother's family in 2006, I had taken on more responsibilities with our children, and Reeve in particular. My regular routine involved taking care of Reeve in the morning, bringing him to school or Yanghoua's video store on Bodart Street in Green Bay,

In October 2005, my family went pumpkin picking at a farm in Kimberly. I have always felt so lucky to be a father. Left to right: Phenix, Sterling, me, Chynna, Reeve, and Maya.

grabbing a coffee at Kwik Trip on my way to work, teaching and doing various scholarship and service work, picking up Reeve on my way home to Kimberly, attending our children's school and community-related activities, having dinner with the family, enjoying some free time with Maya, sleeping, and then waking up to do it all over again.

Amid these personal and professional activities, I had more freedom to slow down and appreciate the quieter moments in my life. I embraced the leaves changing day by day in the fall, the arrival of the first winter snow, the budding of the trees in spring, and the extended daylight in the summer. I watched our children grow. At sixteen, Sterling got his driver's license and began picking up Phenix and Chynna after school.

That fall, despite some uncertainties, I decided to go up for tenure and promotion from assistant to associate professor. I felt confident about my teaching and service, and I had a peer-reviewed article that would be published in December. I had been granted a faculty diversity award from the University of Wisconsin System's Institute on Race and Ethnicity. Plus, I had ten scheduled presentations for the 2008–2009 academic year. Still, I knew I was going up for tenure a year earlier than was standard for assistant professors, and I lacked knowledge about certain institutional practices. The dean had encouraged me to try, but neither of us knew what the outcome would be.

By November, I had completed my file, which included a narrative covering my teaching, scholarship, and service; evidence of my submitted credentials; and supporting letters from students, colleagues, and community leaders. I soon met with the members of the education department's executive committee—a voting body comprised of tenured education faculty—and answered their questions. They voted 5–0 in favor of my tenure and promotion. From there, my file went to Dean Fritz Erickson, who also made a positive recommendation. Next, my file would go to the personnel council, another voting body comprised of tenured faculty from various academic departments and colleges across campus. Because I was leading a study abroad course to Thailand that January, I ended up meeting with them in early February. With all of the positive momentum, I had high hopes.

However, the personnel council voted against granting me tenure and promotion. According to the council, I lacked leadership and my scholarship wasn't distinctive. One council member focused on a student's negative evaluation to highlight everything that was inadequate about my teaching, though the vast majority of my evaluations were very positive. They failed to acknowledge many aspects of my work that mattered to me, including my research on the Hmong American experience, my leadership in establishing field placement partnerships with other school districts, and the positive feedback I'd received from my students. I remained hopeful that the provost and chancellor might still support my case, but I was naive. They, too, voted against my tenure and promotion.

I was devastated. When spring rolled around, someone told

me, "You would have been a slam dunk if you had waited to go up next year." Yet, I did not think my timing was the only reason my case was denied. I believed this was an example of an institution adhering to biased traditions, exhibiting a preconceived distrust of difference, and failing to recognize a unique opportunity to advance the university's mission.

During this period of soul-searching after my case for tenure and promotion was denied, I had another experience that caused me to reflect on issues of identity and belonging. I was at the US Citizenship and Immigration Services building in Milwaukee with my brothers Pheng and Vue. Pheng had misplaced his green card, and we were there to get him a new one. It had been a while since we had spent time together. Kong would have joined us, but he was working at his new job with the Social Security Administration in Wisconsin Rapids.

While Pheng went to check in at one of the windows and Vue left to use the restroom, I observed a stout Hmong man in his fifties accompanied by a Hmong woman around eighteen years old and a child who looked about two. *Is this what I think it is?* I asked myself. After more observations, I concluded that my suspicions were correct. The young woman was this man's niam mos ab, or baby wife. I had heard about the increasing prevalence of Hmong American men in their fifties, sixties, and even seventies returning to Laos and marrying much younger Hmong women, but I had never seen it in person. I was shocked. Little did I realize this would become an ongoing and incredibly controversial issue in the international Hmong community for many years to come.

When Vue returned, we conversed as we waited for Pheng, but I did not bring up the man and his young wife. Vue and I have never talked about religion or politics. Shortly after marrying my sister-in-law, back in the mid-1980s, Vue converted to Christianity. Conversely, Pheng is still very traditional. His world revolves

In the summer of 2009, Maya and I had this professional photo taken in our traditional Hmong formalwear. Dressing in this manner often gives me the surreal feeling of having a dual identity.

around animism and shamanism, much like how our ancestors lived and understood the world hundreds of years ago. Kong and I are somewhere in between. When I am at Vue's place and his family prays, I pray with them. When I am at Pheng's place and his family worships our parents, ancestors, and the good spirits that protect him and his family, I join them. When they're at my place and the occasion calls for a few words, I'll make some nonreligious comments before we eat. Despite our differences, I have always felt that my role is to support my siblings' religious and political beliefs, whatever they may be.

On our way home, after Pheng completed and turned in his paperwork, I couldn't get the concept of a green card out of my mind. Since I became a US citizen about eight years earlier, I hadn't given it much thought. But before I was granted citizenship, the green card meant everything to me, as it allowed me to live and work legally in the country. Back then, I even laminated mine. It was a huge upgrade from the document I had for my first five years in the United States, my ID-94, which wasn't more than a thin sheet of paper the size of a three-by-five index card.

The green card still held that significance for Pheng, even after almost thirty years here. Whenever I asked him why he didn't want to become a US citizen, he would shrug it off without saying a word. I liked to think that was his way of staying connected to our birthland. The United States was not where he felt he belonged. Many years ago, I recognized the importance of US citizenship and its many benefits and privileges, and I decided that I wanted to live my life here. Even so, I knew how Pheng felt. I still wanted to gain a deeper understanding of the land where I was born.

21

With the start of the 2009 fall semester, my tenure and promotion experience had changed my views of university personnel practices but not my loyalty to the noble aim of the university. By mid-October, after consulting with the new interim dean, my department chair, and a few colleagues, I decided to pursue tenure and promotion again. I had come to UW–Green Bay to build an education program that would prepare leaders to serve our schools and communities, and this was still my aim. Also, I hadn't forgotten what some people had said about how I would have had more luck if I had waited another year.

This time around, staying true to institutional precedent, the personnel council unanimously voted for my tenure and promotion. Many of the same members who had previously criticized me now praised my contributions to the education program, the scholarship community, and the university. I was glad to move on, but at the same time, I still felt frustrated by the seemingly arbitrary decisions people were allowed to make on matters so consequential to my life and career. A little honesty and transparency would have allowed me to feel joy over my achievement without a lingering sense of frustration.

In March 2010, with tenure and promotion out of the way, I was able to enjoy myself on a work trip to Manchester College in Oxford, England. There, I met colleagues from various countries to share research about the progress of women throughout history. I was selected to present on the progress that Hmong American women have achieved since arriving in the United States in the 1970s. Their advancements in the fields of education, leadership, wealth, and gender equity have been nothing short of amazing. This research confirmed my belief that opportunities can free people to succeed and to find their rightful place in this world.

I treasured my experience at Manchester College, meeting colleagues from around the world and sharing knowledge. I also enjoyed having authentic English breakfasts, drinking in English pubs, visiting cathedrals and historical sites like Stonehenge and Christ Church Cathedral, watching locals play pickup soccer, and seeing the Magna Carta. Indeed, much of what I had read in my British literature courses turned out to be true.

I also loved being surrounded by many Asian individuals. One day toward the end of my trip, I was shopping when I noticed an Asian woman who I sensed might be of Hmong descent. Though I'm introverted by nature, I gathered my courage and asked if she was Hmong. She said yes, and I was thrilled I'd asked. We conversed about our clans and what brought each of us to England—she was traveling on spring break—before wishing each other well and parting ways. As my colleagues and I walked to our next destination, I reflected on the incredible journey of the Hmong people over the past three decades. From our tribal villages in northern and central Laos, we have made our way to some of the most prestigious academic institutions in the world. I was overjoyed to connect with someone who shared my same beginnings.

After I returned from Oxford, another chance interaction gave me cause to reflect on my teaching career. It was a humid summer morning, and Maya, Reeve, Chynna, my mother-in-law, and I were visiting the Downtown Appleton Farm Market. Since its inception in 1994, the market has brought the city's increasingly diverse residents together and, in doing so, transformed the community for the better. After walking just a block, my shirt was soaked, reminding me of the humidity in parts of Southeast Asia. But seeing the different ethnicities of the vendors and the variety of their wares, along with being in the company of people from all walks of life, pushed my physical discomfort to the back of my mind.

At one point in our stroll around the market, Reeve and I got ahead of Maya and the rest of our group. As we paused for them to catch up, a nearby voice startled me by saying, "Dr. Lor." I turned to see a tall man in his mid-twenties with a thick beard, mustache, and sideburns. I tried to determine whether I knew the person, but my mind drew a blank.

"I'm Matt Peterson," the man said. "Do you remember me?" Then, everything came back to me. I could see him years younger, as a student at Appleton East, without his beard and mustache, wearing faded plaid shorts and a shirt with a Zen logo.

"Yes, of course, I know who you are," I quickly responded. "You were a student in one of my classes many years ago. You and the other Matt. How could I ever forget the two of you?" I recalled how Matt Peterson had been quietly self-assured at a time when most young adults were searching for an identity and trying desperately to fit in. He explained that he was living in the Twin Cities and introduced me to his wife and brother standing beside him.

"Did you end up getting a degree in music?" I asked, recalling his high school dream of entering the music industry.

"Yes, music technology," he explained. "But I'm more into tea now. I'm thinking about going into acupuncture and herbs."

"Wow, that's great," I responded.

"I'm so glad to meet you here," he went on. "After graduation, I moved away, and I wasn't sure if we would ever meet again. I wanted to thank you for being such a great teacher."

"Thank you," I said, moved by his kindness. "Thank you so much for that."

"Yes, you made everyone feel welcomed. And you valued everyone."

I was truly touched. "Your words mean a lot to me," I told him.

We exchanged a few more pleasantries before Matt and his companions departed.

While Reeve happily ate cookies in his stroller, I reflected on my exchange with Matt. Making students feel welcomed and valued was exactly why I had devoted my life to education. I was so grateful he had gone out of his way to connect with me. Teachers don't often get to see the grown students that we put our efforts into shaping. I was sorry I hadn't told him that I had also learned so much from him—in particular, the courage to pursue my dreams.

Finally, the rest of our family caught up with us. They carried bags full of food and flowers. I ordered four stuffed chicken wings from a Hmong vendor. This distinctive Hmong American dish is a creative twist on Hmong eggrolls. The wings are deboned and stuffed with typical eggroll ingredients. On this day, ours were stuffed with vermicelli, lettuce, ground pork, and other spices. Seeing the Hmong vendors and their families reminded me of my time selling meat at a market with my father in Pakay, Laos. As my mind filled with memories of my time in Laos, I thought about how very far I was from my homeland. *Wisconsin is my home now,* I thought. *But will I ever get the chance to see my true home again?*

With my tenure and promotion to associate professor, I had professional stability for the first time since I left Neenah High School in 2005. With that stability, I was able to put my life's routine on cruise control for about a decade. During the academic year, I taught, researched, and provided services to the department, college, and university. In the summer, I took vacations with my family, played soccer, did house chores and yardwork, and fulfilled various cultural obligations.

In 2011, I found time in my hectic schedule to coach the UW–Fox Valley soccer team, and we won both the conference and state

In July 2007, I attended the Hmong Freedom Festival in St. Paul, Minnesota, one of the largest Hmong gatherings in the country. This was my last year playing soccer in the men's competitive bracket at the festival, twenty years after my first appearance in 1987.

championships. Our team didn't do as well in 2012, but we ended up winning the sportsmanship award. This would turn out to be my last coaching experience.

During this period, I also experienced a series of professional achievements. With minimal professional distractions, I established the required credential for promotion to full professor—a request that was approved in summer 2018. Then, to my surprise, my proposal for a sabbatical to work on a manuscript was also approved. And as I started my sabbatical in fall 2018, I also became the Wood Baer Professor of Education, which meant that I would get ten thousand dollars annually to support my scholarship activities for the next five years. Finally, when I returned from my sabbatical, I became the budgetary chair for the Professional Program in Education.

Of course, when March 2020 rolled around, everything went haywire. COVID-19 forced nearly all university functions online, including courses, faculty meetings, field experiences, student services, and student teaching. My days were spent in constant contact with faculty and staff, school districts, and various administrators at the college, the university, and the Department of Public Instruction. Sadly, COVID-19 also forced my siblings and I to cancel the trip to Laos and Thailand that we had planned to take that summer.

In spring 2021, after a very difficult year, I finally celebrated a bit of good news. My first book, *Modern Jungles*, was published, chronicling my childhood journey from the jungles of Laos to Green Bay Junior High School. I had written the first draft of the memoir during my fall 2018 sabbatical. The publication opened the door to a new world of book festivals, interviews, and invitations to speak to middle and high school classes.

By the spring of 2022, though COVID-19 was no longer the threat that it had been, life at UW–Green Bay had permanently transformed. We diversified our student services and course offerings to include in-person, online, and hybrid options, as well as providing classes at many different times of day and even on Saturdays.

At the same time, my home life was changing. Amazingly, our youngest child, Reeve, began driving to high school. It was a bittersweet end to a morning chore that had been part of my routine since our eldest child, Sterling, was five years old back in 1997. For twenty-five years, with a few exceptions here and there, I had been taking our kids to school.

As the fall of 2022 approached, I marveled at the impeccable timing of our children's growing independence, which aligned perfectly with an unexpected opportunity for Maya and me. Reeve, now a high school senior, had blossomed into self-sufficiency, driving himself to school, working, and relying on us less. Meanwhile, Chynna had graduated from UW–Stout, Phenix was in his final year at UW–Madison, and Sterling was completing a data science certificate, also at UW–Madison.

This period of change coincided with the Laotian government's decision to open the Secret War region to tourists, an area that had been closed off since the US involvement in the 1960s. The opportunity to safely visit my birthplace, my parents' villages, and other significant locations from the Secret War era felt like a profound gift.

Returning to my faculty position, I sought financial support from the university for my visit to this previously forbidden region, emphasizing that the visit would be integral to the second memoir I planned to write. I was deeply grateful to receive their full support, including financial backing from the Advancement Office. My plan was to reconnect with my roots and trace the path that I, along with many thousands of Hmong people, had taken in the 1970s on our journey to the United States.

22

After more than forty-five years, I was finally going to visit my birthplace, Long Cheng, Laos. I hadn't been there since around 1977. This time, I was bringing a gift for my parents and ancestors—Maya.

I had been waiting for decades to visit my home region. In the 1960s and 1970s, it was one of the most secret places on earth. Since then, it had been closed to the outside world. Until the summer of 2022, when the Laotian government opened the area to tourism, I believed I would never see it again.

In November, Maya and I flew from Appleton to Chicago, Chicago to Incheon, South Korea, and Incheon to Bangkok. Bangkok had changed a great deal since 1980, when I departed for the United States from Don Mueang International Airport. Back then, it was just on the cusp of becoming an international city, but by 2022, it had become one of the most visited cities in the world. On this trip, Maya and I landed at Suvarnabhumi International Airport.

On the trip to Thailand and Laos I'd taken in 2004, I spent much of my time with professional colleagues and acquaintances, keeping my memories and reflections almost completely to myself. But now, on this trip with Maya, I was in a safe and supportive place where I could truly focus on healing and filling in the missing pieces of my identity. For the first time in decades, we were in our homeland, surrounded by cultures, people, landscapes, climates, cuisines, and languages familiar to us from our childhoods.

As soon as we arrived in Bangkok, I began to imagine what my life might have been if my family hadn't left for the United States. In these alternate realities, I could be running a street food or merchandise cart, washing dishes, cleaning the streets, directing traffic, or driving a taxi, moped, or tuk tuk—if I was fortunate. If I was not so fortunate, I could be living in the slums among millions of people in overcrowded areas, deprived of essential services like running water and proper sanitation. In any of these scenarios, I would likely be dreaming of what I imagined life in the United States to be—a heavenly kingdom filled with happiness, wealth, health, and infinite possibilities.

After several days in Bangkok, we visited Wat Tham Krabok in Saraburi—the same refugee camp that I had visited on my Fulbright-Hays Study Abroad trip. Now, the camp housed only a few Hmong families with connections dating back to 2004. It appeared desolate, bearing little resemblance to its earlier vibrant and bustling life. Maya and I acknowledged that it was another place where we might have ended up. We then visited Chiang Mai, another city I previously visited. In November, the time of my visit with Maya, the mountainous area was stunning and tranquil. Yet we knew that in April, during burning season, Chiang Mai became one of the most polluted cities in the world.

In Chiang Mai, we stopped by Nakornping Tailors, where tailors fit us for a few suits and shirts and promised to have them ready in three days. For the next several days, we explored the night markets, flower gardens, and Hmong resorts, among other local sites and events. Before heading off to Vientiane, Laos, we returned to Nakornping to try on our tailored clothes before shipping them home. That night, we enjoyed a dinner near the Night Bazaar. The young people serving us food—with their hopes, fears, and uncertain futures—reminded me of my youth. As usual, being served made me uncomfortable. I hoped they enjoyed their jobs and knew how much I appreciated them. I also figured, if they were like me when I was their age, they must have thought Maya and I were so wealthy as to be free from financial and personal worries, which was far from our reality.

As Maya and I flew from Chiang Mai to Vientiane, I put in my ear buds and listened to songs from the Secret War and Vietnam War eras—American songs like "Fortunate Son," "Paint It Black," and "(Sittin' On) The Dock of the Bay," as well as Hmong popular songs like "Ntuj Nos Tua Lawm" and "Looj Ceeb." Once we had landed, gone through customs, and exited the airport, we called our Hmong driver, Kham Moua, to pick us up. I had reached out to him through Facebook because I knew from his YouTube channel that he lived in the region where we wanted to travel—an area that attracted few, if any, tourists. Most importantly, he was a mechanic and a good driver, and he seemed to be very knowledgeable about the roads and villages of the area. Kham and his wife, Na Her, traveled all the way from Long Xang to pick us up in Vientiane—quite a drive, especially considering the poorly maintained dirt roads they needed to navigate along the way.

On our four-hour drive back to Long Xang, we passed a section of the Mekong River where many Hmong, including my family, had crossed to seek refuge in Thailand. This was where I lost my mother and one of my two sisters. I was much closer to the site of their drowning than I had been on my visit to the area in 2004.

Maya whispered to me, "Any tears?"

I was feeling many emotions, but I replied, "No, they dried up a long time ago."

Later, we had dinner at Kham's car repair shop before checking into a nearby hotel. We ate at Kham and Na's house again the next morning before departing for Anouvong. Our plan was to retrace the path my family took to reach the Mekong River, stopping in Muang Awe, the last village we lived in before the refugee camp, and spending the night in Anouvong, where my uncle Nhiachue had taught and where some of my siblings had attended school.

When we grabbed lunch at a local restaurant along the way, I had my usual, pad kra pao, a dish of finely chopped pork cooked with chili peppers, garlic, and shallots served with an egg over rice.

Long Xang was another village my family had passed through to reach Thailand—it had been a stronghold for loyal communists. As Maya and I drove through, it warmed our hearts to see students walking, biking, riding mopeds, or being brought home from school by their families. There were a few local markets, ATMs, a bank, and a bus station. The roads in Long Xang were still mostly dirt, rocks, and torn out asphalt. Trucks, buses, cars, mopeds, and people were heading in every direction. For decades, I had longed for an experience like this—being in my homeland where the majority of people around me all shared my cultural background.

As we drove along the dirt road to Pa Lavec, we crossed through part of the route my family and I took on our way to the Mekong River back in 1977. Though I was mesmerized by the beautiful mountains and valleys, I felt no desire to further explore them, as I had vivid memories of being there and simply trying to survive them. Mount Pa Lavec, which I could see through the car window, was used by many Hmong heading to Thailand in the 1970s as a reference point. Men, women, children, elderly people, and even newlyweds had perished there—some from natural causes, but many at the hands of the Hmong communists. In fact, a section of mountains nearby was nicknamed "the Hills of Clothes." Some Hmong communist residents of Pa Lavec and nearby villages cruelly ambushed the Hmong journeying along this jungle corridor, killing them with booby traps, guns, or grenades; taking their valuables; and leaving their clothes scattered on the ground or hanging from tree branches. I spent a moment in silence, paying my respects to all the Hmong who had innocently lost their lives in this region on their way to Thailand.

We finally arrived in Muang Awe. The river, mountains, valley, and other landmarks were just as I remembered them when I lived there. I recalled catching fish and crabs in the river, going grenade fishing with Vue and Pheng, and noticing how the other women hated my mom because she was a widow and therefore threatening to their marriages. I felt incredibly relieved to arrive at this place that had existed only in my thoughts for so much of my life. I had thought I would never see it again.

"Anything I can do?" Maya asked, seeing the pensive look on my face.

"No," I replied. "You have already done so much. You have already healed my soul. And being here is giving me a sense of closure. I can now move on. Thank you for being here with me."

From there, it took us an hour to reach Anouvong, which was once called Muang Cha. I asked Kham why the name had changed, but he didn't know. Maybe the Pathet Lao changed the name in an attempt to erase the history there, since it was the final stronghold of the Chaofa and their resistance. I remembered that Yanghoua and Pheng had lived there with an uncle for a few years and attended school.

The following day, on our way to Long Cheng, we visited an area near Phou Bia just a few miles, if not less, from where my father had been assassinated and buried. After that traumatic event in 1977, my mother, siblings, and I followed the nearby river to Anouvong and then to Muang Awe, our last village before departing for Thailand.

"It must be tough to be so close to your dad," Maya acknowledged.

"It is," I replied. But deep inside, I was also overwhelmed with joy to be close to my father again.

It had taken me decades to learn why the Chaofa leadership had ordered my father's assassination, but in 2020, I had finally learned the truth. Numerous stories from the 1970s had begun to surface. Survivors were sharing their stories with contemporary

I visited the remote area surrounding Phou Bia, the highest mountain in Laos, in November 2022. The US Central Intelligence Agency operated a secret military base here in the 1960s and '70s, and my father was assassinated nearby in 1977.

Hmong storytellers who then shared them through written accounts that ended up on YouTube, Facebook, and other social media platforms. For many months leading up to my father's death on July 16, 1977, the Chaofa in Phou Bia had been deteriorating in resources and in morale. Families and children were starving, with no foreseeable solutions. The Chaofa leadership prohibited anyone from leaving the stronghold to secure outside resources, especially salt, which for health reasons was badly needed. To the Chaofa leadership, seeking outside resources meant surrendering to the communists. Anyone caught bringing in anything, especially salt, without permission from the Chaofa leadership, would be killed without exception. My father challenged the Chaofa leadership because he could no longer stand seeing people starving and suffering. Of course, my father paid dearly, changing the course of our family's life in ways we couldn't have imagined.

In the summer of 2020, a cousin shared with me a handwritten document as evidence of my father's assassination. Since the document was written in Laotian, I later asked Dr. Kou Yang—a professor and scholar of Hmong history and culture at the University of California, Stanislaus—to translate the document.

Report

I, the administrator of the Sub-District of Na Vang, and a witness, want to report to you that Vang Ying Lor, 41, was killed by enemy on July 16, 1977. A bullet from enemy's Carbin rifle hit his chest and he died instantly at 8:30 in the evening at his own home. He was the son of Sia Seng Lor and Sao Va Vang (deceased), and was a resident of Va Ye village, Sub-District of Na Vang, Kou Xay district, Xieng Khouang.

Names of his wife and children are listed below:

Song Mee Lee	age 30	wife
Vang Lor	age 11	son
Vue Lor	age 9	son
Yanghoua Lor	age 7	daughter
Pheng Lor	age 5	son
Lee Pao Lor	age 3	son
Shoua Lor	age 2	daughter
Kong Lor	age 1	son

Remark: We want to state that we are eyewitnesses of the death as mentioned above. We request your consideration in providing needed assistance to the family of the victim as mentioned above.

Va Ye village, July 19, 1977
Administrator of the Sub-District of Na Vang
Yia Dang Vang

Eye Witnesses

1. Yia Chang Vang
2. Cher Tou Xiong
3. Cha Vang Vang
4. Tong Va Lor
5. Fai Tong Lor

My dad's assassination had always been a mystery to me. The document began unraveling that mystery, turning it into a real event with a specific time, witnesses, and survivors—my mom, my siblings, and me. The only mystery left was the identity of the assassin. Given how close-knit the clans and villagers were back then, and how quickly news traveled among them, I have always speculated that people very close to us knew the assassin. However, sensing a concerted effort by those close to me not to reveal the secret, I have come to accept that this will remain a mystery to me. What I know is enough.

For the next two hours, Maya and I traveled along a dirt road through mountains, valleys, and isolated villages until we reached a paved road that wound through the hills and brought us to the outskirts of Pakay. Somewhere in this area was the spot where my mom and I survived the truck accident in my childhood. I had recently heard a version of what happened from someone who came to the crash site shortly after it had happened. He apparently grew up with my parents and knew them well, but he did not know who I was when he was telling the story.

As he explained it, there were two men and two women inside the truck, one person outside hanging onto the door, and a woman and child (my mother and me) sitting in the bedding on top of the transported bamboo. As the truck climbed a steep section of the winding road, the driver started horsing around with the two women, got distracted, and lost control of the truck before he could make it to the top. The truck then started to roll backward and pick up speed. The driver then completely lost control, and the truck went off the road, plunging into the deep valley. The person on the outside of the truck jumped off before it went off the road.

When the man telling the story and some other eyewitnesses arrived at the site of the crash, they found my mother. She had a cut on her forehead and other cuts elsewhere. She then became hysterical and started asking where her child was. Hearing that, the group all started looking for me. They found me a few meters away, untouched. "Not a single scratch," the man said. "It was as though God had picked him up and placed him there as the truck tumbled down to the valley. I had never seen anything like that in my life." The driver survived but spent a couple months in the hospital, and then he had to pay for the funerals of the two women who had perished.

I never did tell the storyteller that I was that child. I didn't want to pollute his memory of the event, and I didn't want to ruin the mystery of who that child became. But maybe, one day, I will.

Once Maya and I arrived in Pakay, we journeyed to the street where my father and I used to hang out at our morning market. My father's meat business was very successful because the many Hmong leaving for Thailand needed meat to preserve for their long journey ahead. I took a moment to reflect on what had transpired here—the ongoing fighting, the assassinations, and the exodus. And the war that continued after we left. I also remembered with sadness the day my mom left our hut, which wasn't too far away, and let the world know of her anger, frustration, and disappointment with my father. While standing in the dirt road, she shouted that my father had been unfaithful. He had a lengthy affair with a widow living on the outskirts of Pakay. This was another reason we didn't leave with the rest of the Hmong fleeing at the time.

From Pakay, we drove to Long Cheng, where General Vang Pao and the US Central Intelligence Agency strategically located their military headquarters. Not only did the location provide safety from the enemy and direct outlets to Vientiane and Thailand, it also had a temple where his military personnel and their families could worship, a house for the king, schools, restaurants, a hospital, and entertainment venues. Sure enough, many Hmong started flooding into Long Cheng in the hopes of starting a new life there. After over a decade in Long Cheng, as indicators of their progress, the Hmong transitioned from being tribal clan leaders to military and civilian leaders, from farmers to scholars, from spiritual healers to nurses, from traditional chanters to rock-and-roll musicians, along with so many other transformations.

As Maya and I walked along the CIA airstrip built in the early 1960s, I couldn't help but think of all that had transpired here in Long Cheng. Many called it "The Nest," as it symbolized the birthplace of Hmong democracy, as well as the revolution against communism and ethnic discrimination. In the distance, I could see the king's house located on the top of a mountain on the southeastern end of the airstrip. In my imagination, I could see my family's house as well. Without money, land, a stable business, or many opportunities for social mobility, our life here was unpredictable and volatile.

Entering the gate of General Vang Pao's military headquarters and taking a few pictures, I thought of my hour-long session with him in 2010 in a hotel in Appleton, Wisconsin. Back in 2009, a group of individuals who were close to the general had approached me about a book project documenting his life. They had chosen me because they knew of my history, trusted my character and values, and felt I would be just and fair in capturing the essence of his life. After going through quite a security check, I finally met him in an Appleton hotel. I could hardly believe I was face to face with a man who had been such a mythical figure to me. We were meeting to determine when it would best for us to talk about his life for the book, and we settled on some times when we could meet in California in the spring and summer of 2011. Our conversation also touched on many other topics, including how he was working with various Hmong people around the world, how he remembered his time as a military general, and why he had dedicated his life to the Hmong and other underrepresented groups in Laos.

"As we were about to leave Laos," he recalled, "I told people close to me that if we ever set foot on this soil again, all the trees that we had just planted will have grown to a point where we won't be able to put our arms around them." Though the general never got to see his prediction about the trees, especially the ones around his military headquarters, I did. Shortly after our meeting, I secured a release from teaching at UW–Green Bay for the spring and summer of 2011, as well as sufficient funding to support the book project. But then as destiny would have it, the general passed away in January 2011.

After the military headquarters, Maya and I visited Som Thong, another formerly peaceful village that became a military base. In Som Tong and Long Cheng, two hundred and fifty thousand Hmong—including boys as young as ten, middle-aged farmers, and older men in their forties—prepared to fight against nineteen million Vietnamese and Laotian communists. Our people were so starved for democracy, we were willing to sacrifice everything to preserve our freedom and identity. A decade of war decimated thousands of soldiers and innocent people. But their sacrifices paved the way for some Hmong to find freedom elsewhere, including places far from these battlegrounds. When the road between Som Thong and Long Cheng was first built, many Hmong envisioned it stretching all the way to Vientiane—a symbol of the path toward a global presence for the Hmong people. And indeed, many used it to get to Vientiane and beyond.

From Long Cheng, Maya and I embarked on a long drive to Phonsavan. The dirt road passed through several of the secluded villages where my parents and grandparents once lived and

A part of my soul was healed in 2022 when I set foot on the soil in Phonsavan, Laos, where this photo was taken six decades earlier, before I was born. From left to right are my mom, my brother Pheng, my sister Yanghoua, a cousin, my brother Vue, my dad, and my brother Vang.

included the route my father would have taken from his village, Has Qhuas, to Phonsavan for business and to visit family members. When we stopped for breaks, I walked along the road, paying homage to the millions if not billions of steps my parents and grandparents once took in order to raise our family and make a living.

It was evening by the time we arrived in Phonsavan. In the mid- to late 1960s, my parents had taken a few photos of our family, including my grandparents, in this village. They must have walked half a day to take the pictures, stayed overnight with family members, and then returned in the morning to their village in Has Qhuas, about twenty or so miles away. Somehow over the last six decades, the photos survived war, jungle treks, river passages, and refugee camps, and ultimately made it to a new world, though my parents did not.

The next morning, before heading off to Luang Prabang, we visited the Plain of Jars—an archaeological site covered with thousands of stone jars dating back as far as 660 BCE. Many of my siblings were born not too far from here, during the war. For many tourists and those born after the war, the Plain of Jars may be simply an item on their bucket list. But for me and many Hmong of my generation and older, the visible damage to the jars caused by bullets, bombs, and grenades mirrors the invisible damage to our souls.

The distance between Phonsavan and Luang Prabang is roughly one hundred seventy miles, but the journey could take days, depending on the weather, road conditions, and accidents. The winding roads, sometimes asphalt and sometimes dirt, snake through many villages and across countless mountains, forests, farms, and terrains. Passing through these places, I speculated about why some people, unlike us, had chosen to stay behind. Based on the information and stories I had heard, I knew a few reasons. Some were afraid the Americans would tax them more than the French. Others had grown tired of imperialistic foreigners occupying their homes and were ready to fight the French, Japanese, or Americans at any cost. Some wanted to retain or even elevate their power, status, and privileges in Laotian society. Others simply didn't know any better or wanted to take advantage of the land and resources left behind by those who had gone.

I wondered if the people who stayed behind had any regrets. I recalled hearing a friend's words that captured my question well: "If you were a Hmong American, would you go back and live in

Laos if you had the opportunity? And if you were a Hmong Lao, if given the opportunity, would you come to the US?" History provides an answer, as a much higher number of Hmong Lao have come to the United States than the number of Hmong Americans who have returned to Laos. Yet, both places felt like home to me, and considering either scenario made me feel emotional.

After a day spent enjoying the markets and architecture of Luang Prabang, as well as nearby Kuangsi Falls, we drove to Vientiane, where we visited the war monument Patuxai, beautiful Buddha Park full of Hindu and Buddhist statues, and a few malls. As I left Laos, unlike my previous visits, I thought that even if I never set foot in my ancestral homeland again, I was content—at last.

23

After our week in Laos, the time came for Maya and I to cross over into Thailand. At the immigration office at the Thai-Lao Friendship Bridge, we said an emotional goodbye to Kham and Na.

"Here's the rest of my kips," I said, handing my remaining money to Kham.

"No, no," he responded. "Take them with you."

"We've no use for them beyond here," I insisted.

"No, no, take them with you for memories."

"I've plenty of memories," I assured him.

He took them, and then humorously added, "You know I was resisting with my words but not with my hand, right?"

We hugged and both had a great laugh.

After passing through immigration, we got on a bus and crossed the Friendship Bridge. Waiting for us on the other side was our Hmong Thai driver, who had come all the way from a village near Ayutthaya. After getting lunch, we drove to the former Nong Khai Refugee Camp site. I wasn't sure how much I would remember of the place where I lived for about a year in 1978, because my memories of my time there feel like a dream.

Years after our family had left the camp, one of my aunts who had been there with me, Vue, Yanghoua, Pheng, and Kong shared her memories of that time with me:

> We were so poor when we got to Nong Khai. I didn't know what would happen to you and your siblings after both your parents had died. That morning after we had crossed the Mekong River, once we learned that your mom and sister had

died, Yanghoua and Pheng cried and cried and cried. You and Kong were too young to know any better.

The Thais who were bringing us to the temporary detention center asked, "Why are they crying so much and not stopping?"

Someone replied, "They had just lost their mom and sister, and their father was assassinated not long ago."

The Thais started crying, too. Everyone started crying. To provide solace, the Thais gave Yanghoua and Pheng some money. They took the money, but they didn't stop crying. And they haven't yet stopped crying.

That evening, Maya and I had dinner in our hotel's rooftop restaurant overlooking Nong Khai, the Mekong River, and Vientiane. We ordered a lot of food—to make up for all those days of starvation during our journey through the jungle to Nong Khai. We ordered fried pork knuckle, salmon salad, seafood soup, papaya salad, and other finger foods, along with a large bottle of Singha. Before eating, I thought, *Mom, Dad, and Shoua, let's share this dinner together*. Though I had not cried over these memories in many years, even Death Valley experiences rain once in a great while.

As we savored our dinner, I reflected on one of the hopes I had nurtured for the longest time. Growing up in the 1980s and 1990s, I had watched talk shows like *The Oprah Winfrey Show* and *The Phil Donohue Show* and witnessed family unions. I had always wished that my mom and sister were just lost, not gone. Being lost meant they could be found. I had hoped so badly that one day I would eventually meet up with them again, like the families on the reunion episodes. But eventually I had to give up on my hope and accept that they were truly gone. The silver lining was that being gone meant they were now with me. Being gone meant they no longer needed to be found. But every day, I miss them—I miss them very dearly.

This 1979 photo, taken as part of our family's relocation to the US, was taken next to our hut in Thailand's Ban Vinai refugee camp. When I visited again in 2022, I stood just yards away from its former location. From left to right are my brother Pheng; my brother Vue; my brother Kong; my brother Vang; Vang's wife, Bao Lee, holding their daughter; me; and my sister Yanghoua.

The next day, we drove to Ban Vinai Refugee Camp, the camp where I lived from 1979 to 1980 and where Maya had lived from 1976 to 1977. We walked around for about three hours, taking in the sights and sounds, reminiscing about our time here, visiting the river and bridge I used to cross, and standing not too far from where we once lived.

Ban Vinai closed on December 9, 1992. The evacuation and the destruction of the community happened quickly. Other landmarks remained, including old concrete structures that could not be looted, the small stream my friends and I used to play around, Mount Vinai, Mount Ten Baht, the soccer field, and the deteriorating Hmong Cultural Temple, which was erected in the 1970s and used until the early 1990s. An official opening of Ban Vinai as a tourist destination had occurred on August 29, 2022, just a few months earlier.

On our way back to Nong Khai, likely traveling the same road my siblings and I did back in 1979, we stopped at one of the street vendors selling fruits—one of our favorite things to do in Thailand and Laos—and purchased a few mangos. So much has changed; yet my memories of the winding road, stilt houses, temples, trees, forests, and village life haven't.

The next morning we headed to Nam Phong, a Thai military base where US pilots picked up the first Hmong leaving Laos in 1975. But we couldn't visit the site due to construction. This was where the general made his last speech to the Hmong before leaving. In the aftermath of the Secret War and Vietnam War, he had become a contentious figure in the complicated political relationships between Thailand, Laos, Vietnam, and the United States. Those present described the speech as heartfelt and somber, as it acknowledged the Hmong people's bleak and uncertain future.

Next, Maya and I visited Phanat Nikhom, a processing facility for refugees being resettled and the place where many Hmong were caged, isolated, and treated like animals before leaving the country. Even with the promise of freedom and a better future, some decided to leave Phanat Nikhom in the dead of night. Despite all the promises of a new life and educational and socioeconomic opportunities, many refugees couldn't accept the reality of moving to an unknown world. For them, the known world was psychologically safer, even if it involved staying in Thailand and being treated as a stateless person or returning to Laos and possibly facing persecution for treason.

The next day's journey was a long, scenic drive to Bangkok. We drove through many Thai towns and villages, noticing how life in these isolated places was vastly different than life in Bangkok and other cities in Thailand. It felt surreal to be here, at Thailand's economic hub, a symbol of prosperity and possibility, where forty-two years ago, I was a refugee about six hours away in Nong Khai.

A few days later, Maya and I arrived at Los Angeles International Airport, rented a car, and drove to Long Beach. My goal was to retrace our three-day bus trip from Long Beach to Green Bay. But this time, I would see it through the eyes of an adult.

We spent a day exploring my old Long Beach neighborhood, the area around Drake Park, the apartment we'd lived in on Magnolia Avenue, and the old Greyhound bus station at the corner of Long Beach Boulevard and East 15th Street. I was reminded of how I didn't speak English during my time here and how I found so many things unfamiliar, including streets, sidewalks, businesses, houses, apartments, and vehicles.

Maya and I visited the Hollywood sign before heading to Fresno, where Yanghoua and my brother-in-law lived for a few years before returning to Green Bay in the late 1980s. In Fresno, we stayed with Maya's niece, Virginia, and her family. She lived with us in Kimberly until 1996 when she got married and moved to Sacramento.

We also visited the resting place of Maya's mom, who passed away a few years earlier. We reflected on how the United States is now home to many Hmong Americans who once wanted to be buried in Laos. Walking through most cemeteries in cities with large Hmong populations, it is now common to see tombstones with the eighteen common Hmong names: Cha (Chang), Chue, Cheng, Fang, Hang, Her (Herr), Khang, Kong, Kue, Lor (Lo, Lao), Lee (Ly), Moua, Pha, Thao (Thor), Vang, Vue, Xiong, and Yang. These tombstones are indications that we've made it—we survived Long Cheng and Som Thong. We've fulfilled General Vang Pao's vision and the hopes of our ancestors, grandparents, and parents. The Hmong language, history, and identity are alive and actively being preserved in communities around the world.

The next day, Virginia packed us a traditional Hmong lunch of boiled chicken with rice, salt, black pepper, and chili sauce as we set out on our ten-hour drive to Phoenix, Arizona. This was our first leg in my attempt to retrace my 1980 bus route from Long Beach to Green Bay. While we may have taken a more northern route through Las Vegas, Colorado, Nebraska, and Iowa, I thought it was more likely we'd taken the more southern route through Phoenix, Albuquerque, Oklahoma City, St. Louis, and Chicago. My first trip had been filled with anticipation and mystery, but this time around, I was able to be more introspective.

We passed Indio, California, and stopped on Interstate 10 to have the lunch Virginia made for us. It was the best lunch I ever had, reminding me of lunches I had back in Laos with my dad. Even after all these years of enjoying various cuisines, including fine dining, nothing compares to homemade boiled chicken with salt, black pepper, and chili sauce. The family connection makes it even more special. I told Maya, "Thank you, Virginia! For the lunch!"

In Phoenix, we ate dinner at a local Thai restaurant. Thai food in the United States is often designed for Western palates, and having just arrived from Thailand, I found the tastes much less fresh. The next morning, we headed to Albuquerque. The scenic views of mountains, deserts, twisty roads, and small towns were transformative for my soul. For years, I'd dreamt of being in this part of the US, and it didn't disappoint.

Our next day's drive through New Mexico, Texas, and Oklahoma was incredible as the road wound through the vast and open land. At the Big Texan in Amarillo, Texas, I had a ribeye, mashed potatoes, and a Coke for lunch. The wide sky and endless horizon gave me a sense of freedom. What a way to live.

We stayed overnight at Yanghoua's home in Wanette, Oklahoma. She'd moved to her trailer home on twenty acres a few years earlier. She shared that there were other Hmong living not too far away. We slaughtered a few ducks and a squirrel for dinner and reminisced about our life back in Laos, where meals often came straight from the forests or fields to the table.

The next morning, we drove up to Vinita to spend a night with Maya's nephew, Josh. He was living with his uncle, who had purchased some land there and was planning to start a business providing materials to the many Hmong who had moved to Oklahoma to seek their riches in the marijuana industry. Our final stop before Green Bay was St. Louis. We had stayed there a few years earlier and tried out a local Asian eatery but found the food disappointing, so this time we opted for steak and salmon. You usually can't go wrong with those options in this part of the country.

In the final stretch, as I had during most of the journey when Maya and I weren't conversing, I reflected on my sense of belonging in this world. I've long thought that most people seem to belong to something, whether it be a religion, political party, club, association, country, or other affiliation, but I have never belonged. It's only recently that I've come to enjoy and embrace this freedom. I've lost and gained so much in my fifty years of life that I've been unsure where I belong or what belongs to me. When I look at pictures of my parents, for example, I know they're my parents, but they're also strangers to me. Similarly, Laos is not my home, yet it is my birthplace—and I yearn for it. Accepting these paradoxes has enriched me in so many ways.

That evening, after we stopped at the last stops on our tour—the old Greyhound bus station in Green Bay and East High School—Maya and I shared how privileged we were to reach a phase in our life where we can reflect on our past. We looked through old photos that we managed to keep safe over the decades—pictures from Maya's times in Ban Vinai; various family members, friends, and relatives; and meaningful places in our lives that no longer exist.

I then came across my graduation program from 1989, one of several items I still have from my high school years. I'd saved it for thirty-three years. The William Ellery Channing quote on the program is, "Every human being is intended to have a character of his own, to be what no others are, and to do what no other can do." I don't remember seeing the quote then, and even if I did, I wouldn't have found any meaning in it. But today, I do.

Epilogue

After twenty years in Kimberly and almost forty-five years living in northeast Wisconsin, I've finally come to appreciate the seasonal changes. In the past, the seasons changed and I hardly noticed as I completed my work and chores. But now, I pay attention to the transformations happening all around me.

In summer, I watch people mowing their lawns, boats creating waves along the Fox River, and kids playing soccer, baseball, and softball in Sunset Park. I cherish the moments when I see deer or foxes walking through our backyard and ducks drifting along the river currents with their ducklings. For me, the summer has become a much-needed escape from the rat race of life, which I am now, more than ever, ready to let go.

When fall comes, I observe the brightly colored leaves fall and scatter across the yards and driveways of our neighborhood. I watch people's clothing change from T-shirts, shorts, and sandals to jackets, pants, and boots, seemingly overnight. And as the hours of daylight get shorter, I recognize the many signs that winter is coming.

Winter in this place has always been difficult for me, as someone born in the tropics, but I have come to recognize its hidden beauty. I like watching squirrels come out to play and dig up the nuts they hid in the fall. From January to April, the river freezes over many times and becomes decorated with beautiful layers of snow. I enjoy the snow but not the shoveling. Two years ago, I finally gave in and purchased a snowblower. For the previous eighteen years, I very much appreciated my neighbors, who helped us with their snowblowers when the snow really piled up.

Especially after a harsh winter, spring never fails to fill me with joy. As trees blossom, their leaves slowly cover the open sky, providing a natural umbrella from the summer heat and sun. I finally stash away the winter gear and open the windows, letting fresh air into the house.

This is the longest I've lived in one place, and we'll stay here for as long as we can.

In early 2023, at age fifty-one, I thought my future was set. Seventeen years into my position as university professor and four years as a budgetary chair, I figured I would teach five more years, maybe publish one more book, and call it a career. Then I would get to spend more time hanging out with Maya and my family, improve my motorcycle riding skills, play soccer, cook, and travel, among other things. I was finally at peace.

But such wishful thinking was short-lived. I kept asking myself, *Is this it for me? Am I at the end of my career? Do I not have anything else to offer society?* I gave in and decided to see if I could contribute to society in a different way. I started applying to a few administrative positions, in Wisconsin and beyond, that I felt matched well with my credentials. One day I got a call from someone at UW–La Crosse, asking if I was interested in the associate dean position at the School of Education. After a virtual interview, I was invited to an on-campus interview with all costs covered by the university.

When the day came, it was snowing hard. If I had been influenced by the culture I was born into, which involved many superstitions and omens, I would have canceled the interview and been perfectly content ending my career as a professor at UW–Green Bay. Instead, I simply switched my car rental from a Chevrolet

Spark to a Colorado. In fact, the falling snow added a spiritual element to my nearly four-hour drive through rural Wisconsin.

The two-and-a-half-day interview was exhausting but pleasant, and I found the staff and environment at La Crosse to be quite welcoming. After meeting with various committees and individuals, I noticed multiple questions regarding leadership style and decision-making, especially in terms of improving faculty and administrative relationships. This led me to believe that, if I were to be offered the position, one of the main challenges of the job would be stabilizing the cultural dynamics within the School of Education.

When I was offered the position a week later, I asked for a week to think through my decision. I knew there would be some sacrifices, including leaving my family, living alone, and navigating a working culture that needed a lot of healing, but I was extremely proud to have been offered the position. Over the years, I'd experienced my fair share of rejections, failures, and moments of doubt, and I knew this opportunity was the result of my persistence and determination in the face of such obstacles. I eventually called the school and said, "Let's make it happen."

In the ensuing days, as I reflected on my seventeen years at UW–Green Bay, I felt grateful to have worked with such generous human beings, who had enriched and transformed my life and career—students, faculty, staff, and community members. I prepared to begin a new journey that I would make alone, in a place far from my family and friends.

Now, as I write this, I have lived and worked in La Crosse for one year. Every Sunday afternoon, or sometimes early Monday morning, I embark on my three-hour commute from Kimberly to La Crosse, and I return home again every Friday evening. As I drive, I listen to Hmong stories and reconnect to the oral traditions of my youth. As recently as ten years ago, Hmong oral

In the summer of 2024, Maya and I recreated the photo we took as newlyweds in 1992 on the shore of Lake Winnebago.

storytelling was nearing extinction, but today, many Hmong use YouTube and Facebook to tell stories just as vibrant as their predecessors' and to reach Hmong-speaking audiences around the world.

Working as an associate dean has reinvigorated my courage to take on new opportunities. But even with a busy work schedule, I have found it challenging to overcome the loneliness and isolation of living far from home. Fortunately, many individuals in La Crosse have welcomed me and, most important, gifted me a sense of belonging.

In my first year, I returned to Kimberly every weekend. The time with my family is well worth the hours on the road. And I also spend my weekends doing things that feed my soul, like riding my motorcycles, attending cultural ceremonies and rituals, playing soccer with old teammates and friends, and sleeping in my own bed. I particularly cherish eating out with Maya at our favorite spots in Appleton—Moon Water Café, Mai's Deli,

Ellinor, and SAP Brunch, Brown Bag, and Bakery. Maya was right when she predicted that the experience would remind us of when we were dating. Our choices in restaurants have improved, but our feelings for each other haven't changed a bit.

At this moment, I feel so humbled by the rich life I've been granted. Over the course of half a century, I've been a son and an orphan; a brother, husband, father, and grandparent; a player and a coach; a dishwasher, janitor, teacher, professor, and administrator; a refugee, a permanent resident alien, and a US citizen. I have lost much of what it used to mean to be Hmong. I can't read or write Hmong, I don't worship my ancestors or spirits, and I don't conduct rituals and ceremonies. But deep down, at my core, I will always be a Hmong kid from the jungles of Laos. In this place, where I was born and forged, I will always be with my parents, grandparents, siblings, relatives, and other Hmong. In this place of my memory, my village is untouched by the outside world, and I look forward to someday exploring beyond the mountains and valleys. It is a place of innocence and joy—and especially a place of wonder. Because everything that has happened to me since I left has been nothing short of an incredible and epic dream.

Discussion Questions

1. The book's title comes from the Hmong phrase *tub ntsuag,* which translates to *bamboo son* or *orphan son* in English. How does Pao Lor reflect on being an orphan throughout the book? In what ways does being an orphan influence his sense of self, even as an adult?

2. Lor's first memoir, *Modern Jungles,* tells the story of his early childhood in Laos, his flight to a Thai refugee camp, and his eventual immigration to the United States. *Bamboo Son* shares the story of his life from age fourteen to fifty-two. Why do you think Lor wanted to write a second memoir? How might the experience of reading this book differ for someone who has read *Modern Jungles* compared to someone who has not?

3. *Bamboo Son* begins on Lor's first day of high school—a day when he experienced feelings of anxiety and inferiority, followed by relief. How might these emotions be considered both universal and specific to Lor's experience? Do you have memories of a first day of school that triggered strong, possibly conflicting emotions? What other times in your life have you experienced similar emotions?

4. A recurring theme in Lor's story is his persistence in the face of adversity. Which instances of his perseverance were particularly notable to you and why?

5. Lor's growth and development as a student, athlete, and professional was influenced by various coaches, teachers, and mentors. In what ways did these individuals nurture and support Lor? In what ways has Lor encouraged the growth and development of others in his life? How has a particular coach, teacher, or mentor influenced your life?

6. Lor describes several traditional Hmong ceremonies and rituals in this book, including weddings and funerals. Which elements of these events stood out to you? What traditions are central to your family or community?

7. At times, Lor found it challenging to maintain his connections to traditional Hmong culture while simultaneously embracing aspects of American culture. What actions did he take to resolve some of those tensions? When have you felt torn between two groups or cultures and what actions did you take to resolve that tension?

8. Lor expresses a great deal of gratitude for his wife and children. How has his commitment to his family influenced his professional career? How do you think Lor's childhood may have affected the choices he has made as a husband and father?

9. Before the Laotian government opened Lor's home region to tourism in 2022, he believed he might never see his birthplace again. At the end of the book, he writes, "deep down, at my core, I will always be a Hmong kid from the jungles of Laos." Is your birthplace significant to your sense of identity? What associations do you have with that place?

10. For decades, Lor had unanswered questions about his father's assassination. In 2020, one of his cousins shared

with him a document that described the assassination, its witnesses, and its survivors. What effect did this document have on Lor? Why do you think he was content to let the identity of his father's assassin remain a mystery?

11. Lor describes two trips that he took to Thailand and Laos in this narrative: one in 2004 with acquaintances on a Hays-Fulbright Study Abroad trip and another in 2022 with his wife, Maya. How did these two trips differ? How did his companions on these trips influence the ways in which he was able to reflect on his past?

12. The subtitle of this book mentions Lor's search for the American Dream. How is your definition of the American Dream similar to or different from Lor's? What associations do you have with the phrase *American Dream*?

13. If you could ask Lor any questions after reading this memoir, what would you ask? Which aspects of his story do you wish you knew more about?

Acknowledgments

Thank you to Maya, our four children, and my siblings and their spouses.

Thank you to the Wisconsin Historical Society Press for the support of this project.

Thank you to Kathryn Thompson, WHSP acquisitions editor, for her belief in my work and the opportunity to write two memoirs.

Thank you to Liz Wyckoff, my editor at WHSP, for her insights and suggestions, which improved the book's clarity and, in many instances, made me reflect more deeply about my journey.

Thank you to Daniel Irvin, for his tireless belief in *Modern Jungles,* dedicating a part of his graduate study to turning it into a screenplay.

Thank you to the Advancement Office at UW–Green Bay and my UW–Green Bay colleagues—Associate Professor and Director of Education Timothy Kaufman; Dean Susan Gallagher-Lepak of the College of Health, Education and Social Welfare; Chancellor Michael Alexander; Provost and Vice Chancellor of Academic Affairs Kate Burns; and Executive Assistant Brenda Beck—who all helped support my research trips to Laos and Thailand that contributed to this book.

Thank you to Kham Moua, our Hmong driver in Laos, and his wife, Na Her, for expertly guiding me and Maya along treacherous roads to revisit some of my former villages.

Thank you to the Wood Baer family for the endowed Wood

Baer Professorship in Education. The funding was critical for *Modern Jungles* and *Bamboo Son,* and I am grateful for their generosity.

Thank you to the faculty, staff, and administrative team at UW–La Crosse for the privilege of a lifetime. My position as the Associate Dean of the School of Education has been the icing on an unexpected and incredibly fulfilling career.

Finally, thank you to anyone I may have overlooked. So many encounters have profoundly impacted me, and I hope my encounters with others have been equally transformative to them.

About the Author

PHOTO BY DANIEL MOORE,
UW-GREEN BAY

Pao Lor is Associate Dean of the School of Education at the University of Wisconsin–La Crosse. Prior to this appointment, he served as budgetary chair for the Professional Program in Education and held the Wood Baer Professorship of Education at the University of Wisconsin–Green Bay. He received his PhD in educational administration from the University of Wisconsin–Madison in 2001. Lor is also the author of *Modern Jungles: A Hmong Refugee's Childhood Story of Survival,* published by the Wisconsin Historical Society Press. He currently resides with his family in Kimberly, Wisconsin.